Sowell
Collection
Books

SERIES EDITORS
KURT CASWELL, KRISTIN LOYD, DIANE WARNER

Also in the series:
The Last Man in Willapa: And Other Poems
by Robert Michael Pyle

Water: Poems and Drawings
by Susan Brind Morrow

THE
WOUND
IS THE
PLACE
THE
LIGHT
ENTERS

HOWARD NORMAN

TEXAS TECH UNIVERSITY PRESS

This book is typeset in Adobe Caslon Pro. The paper used in this book meets the minimum requirements of ANSI/NISO Z39.48-1992 (R1997). ♾

Designed by Hannah Gaskamp
Cover design by Hannah Gaskamp

Library of Congress Control Number: 2024945061

ISBN: 978-1-68283-238-7 (paperback)
ISBN: 978-1-68282-239-4 (ebook)

Texas Tech University Press
Box 41037
Lubbock, Texas 79409-1037 USA
800.832.4042
ttup@ttu.edu
www.ttupress.org

For Madalyn Marcus

CONTENTS

ILLUSTRATIONS

THE
WOUND
IS THE
PLACE
THE
LIGHT
ENTERS

CHAPTER 1

THE WOUND IS THE PLACE THE LIGHT ENTERS YOU

I was raised to believe that Eternity resides in the past. This memoir is about the formidable, never not gratifying qualities of friendship with the painter Jake Berthot, one of the most singular and compelling souls I ever met. It is a book about our friendship's constancy, its vexations, just the times hanging out together, endless talk, driving to look at a particular tree at dusk, personal tragedies, lots of letters sent between us. The memoir essentially takes place during the evening, sleepless night, and following morning of my final visit with Jake, November 26–27, 2014, at his home at 107c Ricci Road in Accord, New York. On December 30 of that year, when I received the phone call from Verna Gillis (whom Jake called "my guardian angel"), she said, "This will break your heart. But I need to tell you that Jake died at home this afternoon. I know you were scheduled to drive up tomorrow." My first thought was that I shouldn't have left in the first place. Throughout these pages, various incidents and extended anecdotes from the previous thirty-two years are woven into the framework of that final visit. An aphorism from Ovid speaks to my attempt at an abiding sense of mortality: *Even while we speak the hour passes.*

3

Jake had many devoted friends. As in most lifetimes, certain of Jake's friends fell away. The phenomenon of friendship itself, directly or by indirection, was not an infrequent subject for us. Still, I didn't personally know anyone in the closest orbit of Jake's painter friends, nor did I know any of his non-painter art world friends, such as the famous critic Dore Ashton, who spoke at his New York memorial; I have read the affecting Berthot–Ashton correspondence in the Archives of American Art, Smithsonian Institution. ("If anyone again calls me a 'painter's painter' . . . I think I'll scream!") He spoke with me about the grief and pain he felt when that friendship frayed. ("We were dear family friends. She didn't think I should be painting trees. It got complicated. My painting changed, her ideas about my painting couldn't. But even that's too simple a way to put it.") He spoke with me often—very often—about his deep connection with neighbors, Soundscape record producer Verna Gillis and splendid jazz trombonist-composer Roswell Rudd. He spoke about painters Philip Guston (who bequeathed him tubs of cadmium red), Milton Resnick, Max Gimblett, and Harvey Quaytman; he gave me a small painting by Quaytman for my fifty-fifth birthday, a tremendous surprise. One evening, Jake delivered a veritable disquisition on Naoto Nakagawa's *Sand Painting (for Pueblos)*. He spoke about his former gallerist David McKee. He spoke about the poet Gregory Orr, affectionately citing Greg's essay, "Turnings and Returnings: The Art of Jake Berthot." To say he spoke often about another guardian angel, Betty Cunningham (see the afterword, "Betty"), of The Betty Cunningham Gallery, would be to say that there are stars in the sky. Anyway, friendship meant a lot. It meant the world.

I first met Jake when my wife, the poet Jane Shore, introduced us in March 1982, when we stayed at his loft/studio on Bowery in New York. Jane had met Jake in New York art and literary circles.

4

My first letter from him is dated April 26, 1982. Throughout the years, never more than two months went by without letters being exchanged between us. At one point in 2001, taking into consideration how often he had sketched trees in their margins, Jake referred to this as "trees of the epistolary life." I got to know Jake best when he moved to Accord in the late 1990s and began to paint and draw trees. It seemed that the effects of the Hudson Valley landscape, the Catskills region, allowed him a longed-for source of introspection and in turn perhaps less guarded emotions. "I feel more myself here," he said. "I like my life a lot here. I like taking care of this house."

My own "Jake Berthot Notebooks," both piecemeal and formal chronicles of visits with Jake, amount to fifty-four notebooks of one hundred pages each. A view frequently promulgated has it that soon after his relocation (which he called a "recentering") to rural surroundings, Jake's work changed from *abstract* to *figurative*. But that is not how Jake saw it.

> "... *okay* ... *if you're going to use the term* ABSTRACT *to begin with* ... *then* ... *in some ways* ... *the trees are as abstract as anything I've ever done* ... *it's just that the subject matter is*

so identifiable. . . . I don't see any contradiction. . . . Besides, it's not semantics . . . it's emotion . . . it's spirit . . . (Letter, December 4, 2001)

The thing was, when I saw Jake's earliest paintings and drawings of trees, I knew a profound sea change had taken place. Yet, for all of my own noticing, of course I could never fully comprehend the volumes of sheer thought, let alone innumerable hours of painting and drawing that it took to manifest the fullest devotion to trees, which was unabated and evolving right up to the end. However, I do know that there was a kind of unifying philosophy in what he often said of his trees, "I want to paint the silence before it disappears."

A gift from Jake is a sketchbook containing thirty drawings of the same birch tree, one drawing per page, each seeming to materialize from the mist; some have smudges of black that resemble billows of coal smoke. This sketchbook is from 2011, and I remember our driving to Minnewaska State Park Preserve to look at this very birch. I made a map; I could find that birch today, if it is still standing. Small thing, maybe, but a fond memory, just after dusk Jake asked me to take the wheel, and on the passenger side he worked on a drawing of that birch tree the entire way home.

In reviewing my own journals, photographs of Jake's studio, and letters, I can name works—a kind of visual coterie—whose presence in reproductions on his walls, or lying around on one table or another, allowed him to be "haunted by trees of the past," as he put it. There were van Gogh's *Autumn Landscape at Dusk, The Poet's Garden, Orchard Bordered by Cypresses,* and especially the pencil, charcoal, pen and ink and white opaque watercolor, *View of a Wood.* There was *Saint Sebastian Succored by the Holy Women* by Corot. There was the entire 1994 collection of photographs by Robert Adams, "Cottonwoods," which included a line

from Edward Thomas that Jake copied out in a notebook, "Trees and us—imperfect friends." There was *Interior of the Forest During Winter* by Karl Bodmer. There was *Tahiti Landscape* by Matisse. Of works by Cézanne, there were *Studies of a Tree* and *Tall Trees at the Jas de Bouffan*. There was *Dutch Landscapes with Farmsteads* by Rudolf Ribarz and *Tree Studies* from a notebook of Egon Schiele's. There was Monet's *The Bodmer Oak, Fontainebleau Forest*, and there was Vuillard's *Woman Seated in a Garden*, and there was Soutine's *Landscape at Céret*, and there was Ogata Kōrin's untitled panels of winter trees, from the early 1700s. Jake greatly admired the "Murier Blanc" series of aquarelle, crayon, and pastel drawings of trees by Farhad Ostovani. And then there were the two works "I maybe gaze at most often of all"—a foreboding stand of trees in *Stone Pines* by Inness, who so deftly in his landscapes rendered the very early or very late daytime hours. And secondly, a photograph (photographer unknown) taken in Asnires and attributed to 1887, that pictures Émile Bernard and, with his back to the camera, Vincent van Gogh. "*The whole effect . . . but the tree in particular . . . just really gets to me,*" Jake wrote in a letter dated February 18, 2012.

And here I am about to become a docent in my own farmhouse.

On a living room wall is a 26-inch x 20-inch drawing of an oak, which Jake drew in 2002; he had sent this drawing in September 2003, a few months after an unspeakable incident took place in my family's house in Washington, DC. Our house sitter, a 40-year-old woman who used her verse to create a garish personal mythology of her childhood and immigrant life, murdered her 15-month-old son and then took her own life. My family had been spending the summer in our Vermont farmhouse. Sent with the drawing was a letter in which Jake had written, "*. . . your lives have been wounded . . . The Wound Is The Place the Light Enters You . . . (Rumi) . . .* PRAYERS FOR YOU, JANE, EMMA *. . . hope this tree . . . is solacing . . . a solace . . .*" After this sordid incident, Jake made three straight weeks of nightly telephone calls, "just checking in." He also sent three volumes of the works of the poet Rumi.

In the large guestroom upstairs are *Study for River Maple* (see "The Refutation of the Biographer") and an untitled drawing of a tree of which Jake wrote, "I consider it . . . a kind of . . . reincarnation-variation . . . etc. . . . of Stone Pines." And in the hallway, there is a triptych of birch trees, whose title is, *Oh to join a procession of ghosts going somewhere known only to them to take the mystical waters,* a quote from Edward Lear's *Indian Journals, 1873–1875.*

We live indoors among all these trees.

On a sun-glinting-off-snow and bitterly cold morning a year to the day after Jake died, I was looking out the wide kitchen window of my family's 1830s farmhouse at birch, maple, beech, willow, oak, and butternut along the meandering stone wall, and farther out to the forested ridgeline. Finally, I shifted my gaze to the bare trees near the three-story barn and realized, with startling clarity, that what I was seeing were Jake's trees. What I mean is, I had to work my way through Jake's drawings in order to reach the actual trees in the world. This phenomenon continued all through that winter, subsiding during the following spring, summer, and autumn. But in December 2016 it returned and has returned as early as November every year since. And now I find myself gratefully anticipating this. What is more, I have become quite comfortable in the belief that when I see Jake's trees everywhere on the farmhouse property, it is a perpetual aspect of mourning.

CHAPTER 2

ANGELS

"I'm *human* because I'm still breathing and can look out at trees, but I'm not a *being* because I can't get to my studio and work. *Human* but not *being*." This was a heart-rending refrain. It was also literally true that Jake felt physically too weak to make the twenty-yard journey from house to studio. Though after we talked all night, at around 8:30 a.m. he finally made it out there.

My friend, the painter Jake Berthot, died of leukemia on December 30, 2014, at age seventy-five. He died at home, 107c Ricci Road, in the town of Accord, in the Catskills region of New York. The last time we saw each other, I had arrived just before dusk. I brought potato-leek soup and a baguette. I walked right into his house. Its architecture perhaps more defined a cabin. Inside, an uninterrupted living space, bedroom off to the side, but definitely also a working space. *Haimish,* the Yiddish word for homey warmth, lived in, welcoming. Jake's own drawings on the walls and on tables, a painting by Milton Resnick here, a drawing by Philip Guston there, a solid cast-iron wood stove, leather Eames reading chair, worktable, bookshelves spilling over, organized clutter. How many hundreds of hours had I spent there? It was to me an intimate space, and no less vivid and immediate in memory now. Outside, Jake had inventively landscaped, cleared trees, planted a garden. I enjoyed working in that garden and talking. Wood was stacked on the back porch. From the front steps you could see the studio, which always seemed as large as the house, and in square footage may well have been. Both were painted gray. It all lived up to what Walter Benjamin called "a preoccupied home." In this case, preoccupied by art.

When I entered the house, I saw that Jake had dozed off sitting upright on the futon sofa. It sounded like he wasn't breathing so well. His face looked a little pale, with an archipelago of splotches on his forehead, as if he'd had some sort of allergic reaction. He was wearing a dark-green flannel shirt, well-worn fleece vest, brown corduroy trousers, thick socks, ratty slippers. He'd fallen asleep with his reading glasses on; a book had fallen to the floor. The wood stove was down to ashes, so I lit some kindling and set in two logs. I went out and set my overnight bag on the quilted bed in the guest room, which was under the same roof as the storage racks of paintings and cabinet drawers full of drawings and the spacious studio itself. But as it turned out, I didn't ever unpack.

Jake woke at about 5 p.m.; seeing me he said, "I'm a human, but not a being." I went into the kitchen. "Did you bring potato-leek?" he said.

"Your wish was my command," I said. I warmed up the soup a little and set a bowl, along with a piece of bread, on the low table in front of him; I sat in the Eames chair with my own soup and bread. He asked after my wife Jane and daughter Emma.

"You look pretty good, Jake," I said.

"I look like shit," he said, "and you look like you haven't slept in a week."

"Now that we've got the compliments all out of the way," I said. I set my bowl aside and walked over; without his standing up, embraces; kisses on the check. *The Collected Poems of Wallace Stevens* was on the table, *The Testing Tree* by Stanley Kunitz, *Emily Dickinson: Collected Poems*, *Adventures of the Letter I* by Louis Simpson, a volume of Emerson's essays, too. He said, "I've been thinking again, maybe for the ten thousandth time, about that Emerson idea—"

I sat back in the Eames chair. "Every natural fact is a symbol of some spiritual fact."

"Yes," he said, "but I'm not going to live long enough to completely understand it. But I've come to believe that's what I was trying to get to with every single tree I drew. Or painted. Trees as spiritual facts . . ."

"Have you been reading Emerson again?"

"Yeah, his essay on friendship—it's not his best. But still beautifully written."

"Complicated subject," I said, "friendship."

"Very complicated."

"Do you think we have a complicated friendship?"

"By all means. Look at the two of us—how we are. How could we not? But the complications somehow never forestalled the friendship itself, is how I see it."

"Why did you just now say 'forestalled'? That's past tense."

"I didn't mean it that way," he said. "Don't get all worked up—I'm not going to die while you're here. I'm still present tense."

"What have the last few days been for you?" I said. "You know, since we last talked on the phone."

"Well, this illness ain't a barrel of laughs. Fitful sleep. If I sleep. Not peaceful dreams. Listen to a lot of music. My friends Verna and Roswell are my guardian angels—Roz brings his trombone down and I play drums. He's a genius jazz composer, as you know. I listen to the radio. I seem to fade in and out. Stamina yesterday was low, today's maybe a little better. It's up and down like that. But then some days, I'm so clear-headed it's almost—"

"—like nothing's wrong."

"Well, that's the deception of the brain. But the body's more honest."

"You've had a lot of visitors—that been okay?"

"I don't know. What's that Merwin line, something about a procession of farewells . . . anyway, Verna's been on top of appointments, but actually I end up canceling half of them. Just not up to it. I use the time alone pretty well, I think. Depends if I can concentrate on reading. I just can't feel I'm a *being*, you know?"

I went over and sat next to him on the sofa. "Jake, I can easily arrange to move in here for a while."

"I'm not afraid of dying alone, if that's what you're worried about."

"Well, it's a matter of keeping each other's company."

"I've never died before. I don't know if I'm doing this right."

"Yes, you've never died before, how am I doing as a friend with that?"

"By definition, I guess we're both amateurs."

As the hours progressed, it was impossible not to understand that Jake was in a kind of fugue state of philosophical agitation. At long stretches he was all non sequiturs. For instance, when I said, "Do you want some tea?" he responded, "I've read a lot lately about morphine. *Good-bye to All That*—Robert Graves, World War One stuff. There's a lot of morphine in it."

"Sure, I've read that book," I said.

"Do you think any of my shirts will fit you? I've got one I wore to the Venice Biennale."

There was a lot of this sort of exchange. We needed a subject to organize emotions. On a nearby worktable was a light brown, hardcover journal; on the cover was scrawled ANGELS. I set it on the low table in front of the sofa. I set the cassette recorder there, too. "Want to record some more?" I said.

He nodded yes. "Why not let's talk about the angels you drew."

I could almost see full alertness return to his face. "That's a good idea," he said. "I'm up for that subject. I'll have another cup of coffee." Which I right away got for him. "Whose posterity are we recording for this time, anyway?"

I didn't quite know how to answer that. He took off his vest, replacing it with an old sweater. He leaned back against the pillows on the sofa. His cat was curled near the woodstove. Earlier it had been chasing a weasel that had found its way into the house. I turned on the small high-definition Romacci tape recorder, which I bought since the original recorder we'd used for two years had broken down.

We paged through the notebook. It was full of sketches of angels. (I am looking at it now.) Throughout were quotes from Sappho, Rumi, Issa, Adorno, Saint-John Perse, Rilke, Dickinson, Cavafy, Merwin. Jake had always been an inveterate reader of poetry. His poetry books were all marked up; underlines, notes in the margins. One of my favorite things he wrote on a drawing: *I'm exasperated with Rilke; next day I'm back with Rilke.* Like an entry in a diary about an old love-hate relationship.

Even gaunt and depleted, Jake was one of the handsomest men I'd ever seen, though of course it was only natural, within the insistences of memory, now and then to superimpose his former physical appearance onto his present one. "A Sam Shepard type," my friend Kazumi, who had seen Jake at some art opening or other, said of him. That *human* and *being* stuff was so much about his studio —he just couldn't make it out there. We tried twice between 6 p.m. and 8 p.m. The first time, he collapsed back onto the sofa, and said, "I'm not a being," and slept for a few minutes; the second time, we got his overcoat and shoes on and made it to the door, but that didn't work out, either: ". . . look, this is a particularly bad day physically." On the sofa again. More coffee. Then we blasted Bob Dylan's *Blonde on Blonde.* "'Leopard-Skin Pill-Box Hat' always cracks me up," he said, "—but doesn't the whole album bring so much back? God, it's overwhelming sometimes. This one friend of mine once told me, back in the day, he put *Blonde on Blonde* on the turntable, trying to impress his girlfriend, you know? Turned out, she didn't really want to have anything to do with him for the rest of the night. He'd been completely replaced. She'd much rather hear what Dylan was saying over and over. She liked Dylan's *mind*, you see. I love that he told me that story. Such a great '60s moment, right?"

Sitting next to Jake, I was intensely aware of something unsettling but I couldn't seem to define it, or stop the inevitability of it. While in the moment, taking in Jake's face in profile, I was at the same time experiencing a sense of elegiac anticipation—how will I feel when my friend is gone? I tried to shake this off and failed. Right then and there, I understood something of what haiku master Matsuo Bashō had written when, in 1689, along a mountain path in northern Japan after months of walking, he looked over at his travel companion, Sora, and thought, *which step had turned us toward the next life?*

There were two books of Albert Ryder's paintings on a table. The arrival of dusk outside replicated the spectral atmosphere of some of Jake's paintings of landscapes, which he'd done over the last fifteen or so years. Replete with fugitive shards of white in an otherwise dark or darkening landscape, lingering ghosts of daylight. Just a splotch or faint glow here and there. For instance, the painting finished in 2001 that is titled *Approaching Night (for Ryder)*, with a tree on the left side of the canvas, the rest filled with a golden dusk –right there you could see Jake putting his love for and knowledge of Ryder on exhibit. Owning up to it. The crepuscular density and unease. Like in so many of Ryder's, these landscape paintings of Jake's filled my heart with portent. Intensity of thought and beauty incarnate in the painted orchestration of these elements, all sponsored by Jake's insistent melancholy. "I like to think that making those landscape paintings was the transforming of melancholy into paint, in a way," he'd said a decade earlier. "Though that's not it entirely. It's never just one thing." Now the cat jumped up and settled on Jake's lap. "What's that line you love so much," he said, "—from that guy who wrote *Rashomon?*"

"Akutagawa Ryūnosuke," I said. "'What good is intelligence if you can't discover a useful melancholy.'"

"Yeah, that's it. *Useful melancholy.* Question for me is, how to put it to good use. What emotion am I supposed to have while dying? Maybe melancholy is just right for that. Melancholy needs its own parameters. You know, the size of a canvas."

Now he showed me a slide of a drawing. I held it up to the lamplight. It was done in ink wash and Gesso on paper; its dimensions were 28 1/2 x 20 5/8 inches. It was composed in two levels of sepia and black; there are three angels, one aloft, literally sitting on a cloud, and two are earthbound—one of the earthbound angels is somewhat obscured or, as Ryder put it, "enclouded" in black. Written in cursive along a divide are the opening lines of "The Death of God," a poem by Stephen Dunn: *When news filtered to the angels, they were overwhelmed by their sudden aloneness.* (In our telephone conversation, Stephen Dunn said, "By news, I meant news of the death of God. The angels get that news, and a precise kind of loneliness arrives.")

"I made that drawing in 2007, I think it was," Jake said.

"It's got both figurative and abstract elements," I said. "But it's not part of the Artist-Model series. Those were done between 1986 and 2006."

"I know when they were done! But the truth is, I'd been drawing angels for years. Even in the margins of all those letters I sent you."

"Yes, lots of angels in the margins. How did you consider the figures of angels? What thinking went into that? I'm being an interlocuter here, Jake—don't give me that look. I'm actually curious. I want to know."

"It's like with any drawing for fifty years," he said. "You just put it on the wall, sit in a canvas chair, gaze at what you've done, and try to think it through. It might take days or weeks or months. As for angels, I figured that the theological provocations would be different for different people. You could doubt the existence of angels but you couldn't doubt the existence of angels in the drawing. But mainly I was interested in angels as *figures*, getting the lines right, the technical stuff of drawings. Some are aloft, right? You need to think about the space around a figure aloft."

"But looking back—"

"Okay, right, well, my study of the figure of angels began when I first started painting, really."

"This is the first time we've talked about this subject, now that I think about it," I said.

"Okay, well, let me give you an example. What comes to mind —wow, I haven't thought of this in ages. This seventeenth-century epic poem—I can't remember how I discovered it. Actually, I think it may have been from Milton Resnick, in the Village, what year? The sixties. Or maybe from a poet that my first wife Jenny knew. I can't quite remember. The seventeenth-century epic poem was written by someone named Heywood. Title was, "Hierarchy of Angels" but it wasn't so much the poem as the engraved plates that went with it. I remember thinking of those angels . . . choreographically, in a way. Some were radically tilted, high in the air, like they couldn't hold their balance. Falling. In a contorted kind of way. Like an Egon Schiele contorted figure falling. I remember that some of the angels looked bored, or uninterested, but others seem to have this look of astonishment—and a couple looked frightened. Of what who knows? I remember in one of the engraved plates was an angel that had a striking resemblance—in the construction of its face—a striking resemblance to my father. That freaked me out. I didn't know what the hell to make of that! Let's see, what else? There's a line from some Polish poet, *Until you lowly eaters of bread will be made into angels*. I did a couple of drawings inspired by that line. Byzantine and Medieval angels, into the Renaissance. Fra Angelico's *The Annunciation*. The classical erotes or putto from the Italian Renaissance. I mean, I didn't question the theological assumptions behind these works. I studied them as paintings. Like any good student of art must."

"Which others are you remembering right now?"

"The Archangel Gabriel in a deacon's vestments—that Dutch masterpiece, Jan van Eyck's—I think it's titled *The Annunciation*. That's fifteenth century. And I love so many of the Persian angels,

angels in Mecca. They're really beautiful works. I like Chagall's *Jacob's Dream*. I think I saw that in a museum in Nice. Angels all over that canvas. Giotto's *Crying Angels*. I mean, you look at the expression on the faces of Giotto's angels in that painting—it's like the whole range of human emotion. Or maybe some emotions people no longer even have expression for. Expressions only angels could have—something like that."

"I'll put on some tea, okay?"

"Off the meds I just start talking like this. Sometimes the meds jazz me up. But sometimes off the meds I get jazzed up. I just start talking and talking—I mean, what expressions am I referring to on those angels?—expressions from a past time, expressions people forgot how to even show on their faces anymore. Early fourteenth-century expressions. But also there's that Wim Wenders movie, *Wings of Desire*. I drew a lot of angels because of that movie. Jesus, that flick really got to me."

"Let's watch it again."

And so we did. I had watched it with Jake years earlier and figured he probably still had the DVD on some shelf or other. I put more wood on the fire. I found the DVD and set it all up and we didn't say a word for the duration of the film, which ran two hours and eight minutes.

The story is set in post–WWII Berlin. The narrator is an angel played by Bruno Ganz. Ganz's immediate cohort angel is played by Otto Sander and I see the film in part as a depiction of their friendship under the strangest of circumstances. Though the story can't be summarized in any way that does it justice, these two characters are more or less on assignment to eavesdrop on mortals and invent ways to comfort them in their quotidian distress. The whole thing is shot by cinematographer Henri Alekan dominantly in sepia-toned black-and-white. At times the soundtrack sounds as if it is being mumbled and hummed by Marlene Dietrich suffering the rapture of her most disconsolate hours.

The screenwriters Wim Wenders and Peter Handke declared that they were influenced by Rilke's "desperate lyricism" and Homer's "angel of storytelling." At one point Bruno Ganz falls in love with a trapeze artist played by Solveig Dommartin, whose loneliness, especially when she is depicted aloft on a trapeze, is precisely what inspired Jake's drawing, *When new filtered to the angles, they were overwhelmed by their aloneness*. "She's aloft, but can't seem to rise above her own earth-bound sadness," Handke wrote. Anyway, Solveig Dommartin is so consuming an object of desire for Bruno Ganz that he becomes mortal so he can experience all the tactile and sensory human pleasures again, and hopes to share love with the trapeze artist. So it is a romantic tragedy, a near-theological melodrama, and a kind of monochromatic symphony on screen. When the film ended, Jake said, "Anyone who thinks this is all about death is crazy—it's about the nature of being alive."

"So, the Bruno Ganz angel is *being*—but he wants to be fully *human* again."

"Yeah, and it's so goddamn heartbreaking, really. And so dark, but so full of surprising light, too. I mean, the city seems desperate for light. Ganz and Otto Sander seem desperate for light, for it to enter them, somehow. It reminds me of—"

Jake stood up, the cat scattered off, knocking over Jake's teacup. He more or less shuffled over to a nearby bookshelf. He found a collection of poems by the thirteenth-century Persian poet, Rumi. He sat back down on the sofa and paged through, "Where is that? Where is that?" and finally found what he was looking for.

He read, "The wound is the place the light enters you."

CHAPTER 3

THE REFUTATION OF
THE BIOGRAPHER

W e listened to Chopin nocturnes and preludes. "The last music I'd love to hear would be the nocturnes," Jake said. "But the only way to guarantee that happening would be to have them playing day and night—when I kick the bucket, Chopin would play me on to the next place. If there is one." Time sifted by. Not much talking. I paged through books about Ryder. Jake slept a little. He woke and said, "I've got all this desire and willingness, I look through a book of Cézanne's, the inspiration is there. I did a sketch—the pencil felt like an anvil. Want to see it?" He showed me a piece of drawing paper; overlaid on a grid was an oak tree, branches spread wide. "This tree's right off the back porch. It took me four or five nights. It's basically an insomnia drawing, in a way. But mostly I can't work well in the house. Here, take it home with you—an end-of-days tree."

End-of-days tree.

I prepared some more tea. "That little catnap I just took's given me some juice, man," Jake said. Then roughly between 9:30 p.m. and 11 p.m. Jake drew on what seemed a miraculous deep well of energy. Our mercurial conversation went from Jake's snappish, contrarian treatment of a visiting Dutch art critic, to a eulogistic paragraph written by the Swiss playwright Max Frisch, to

23

Jake's drawing, *The Model's Negotiation, or David Hockney Meets Elizabeth Taylor*. All of our ricocheting banter seemed to create its own logic of progression which I willingly gave into. Besides, I was just happy to be there. Yet there was this one moment, while we briefly reprised the experience with that Dutch fellow, that Jake got so riled up that I said, "You're having a conniption fit," words he particularly loved to pronounce with an exaggerated Yiddish accent. "Yeah, well," he half-shouted, "I'd rather die by conniption fit than goddamned leukemia!" Which was funny and not so funny.

There was another kind of finessed negotiation, too. More than once, if I felt a precipitous escalation of mood, I'd say, "Jake, maybe we should let it rest for a minute," and he'd reply, "No, we really need to talk about this." As if he wanted me to comprehend that conversation was a way to "measure out mortality." (That phrase from Jake's mentor, Milton Resnick.) Indispensable hour by indispensable hour, to measure out mortality. But none of this felt in the least dramatic; it simply felt once-in-a-lifetime. And that was quite enough to feel.

As anyone who'd spent time with Jake certainly knew, he could get downright loquacious, especially when intoxicated by a particular subject—take Cézanne's landscapes, for instance, or what he once called "the eclectic melancholy" of Ryder. Really about any subject under the sun: books, film, gossip about neighbors or the art world. That is, not timid of impassioned discourse. His speech—the sound of his voice—was deliberate, pitched to different octaves by different moods, and some words were almost drawled. Going by a number of his YouTube interviews or appearances, you wouldn't necessarily deduce that he could be so gabby; some of those contain epigrammatic soliloquies, and definitely a kind of vigilance toward spouting platitudes about art. (Though there are occasions when there's an offhanded humor, too.) While always deeply thoughtful, Jake often seems to be alert to a quote from Thomas Hardy he'd scrawled on a page in a sketchbook, *Beware the capacity for a casual utterance to become an epitaph.*

On the telephone, he preferred, at least with me, late-night conversations. Sometimes he'd play me a pop song. I recall his playing "American Tune" by Paul Simon, and his singing along with the line, *I don't have a friend who feels at ease.* "Do you?" he said.

"Do I what?"

"Have a friend who feels at ease."

"Not any of my dearest friends," I said. "Not if we're talking in the existential sense."

"Did it ever occur to you that's *why* they're your dearest friends?" he said. "But me either, no friends that are at ease. Not really. And I'm talking in every sense."

I recall one time we chatted away on the phone for nearly three hours—during which we each set our phone down in order to prepare a cup of coffee—and finally we recognized, and were amused by, the fact that we'd collaborated on usefully filling up some of an insomniac night, and then we talked about our individual and frequent bouts of insomnia; we each gave our fullest insomniac resume, and recollected origins of it in childhood. Jake said he could remember his first sleepless night, whereas I couldn't remember mine. "I've been looking closely at that collection, "Insomnia Drawings," of Louise Bourgeois you sent me," he said. "I think I'm starting to get what's going on in those. She wrote so well, too. Most painters can't write for shit. Rackstraw Downes can. Agnes Martin can, though she can be a touch sanctimonious. Twombly. But Louise Bourgeois, she wrote so honestly. She was prolific, too. She revealed a lot in her writing. All that father stuff. Put all of her writing together, you get an amazing autobiography of a sort. Though I haven't thought this through, you know?"

According to my journals, it was on a bitter cold night in January 2011—me in my farmhouse library, Jake in his studio—we had a contretemps, as I prefer to call it, about a poem by Donald Hall. I knew Jake liked Hall's writing a lot; me not so much. But when he'd read this particular poem to me over the phone, I said that I recoiled from the poet's need to be so publicly identified as an iconic widower—I felt it was solipsistic grief, and undignified, to my way of thinking. Where had that come from? I felt as if my embittered response to the poem had catapulted out of me. Laughing, Jake said, "Look, if you have an opinion, don't hold back." But then he loosed a brief salvo of disappointment, that I was so closed-off about how "honest and raw" the poem was. "This doesn't reflect well on you," he said.

"Probably most things don't," I said.

"Well, try being wrong this time."

Over the years, it was exceedingly rare for us to have such a severely opposite take on a work of literature. When he'd proselytize a poem –Wallace Stevens's "Solitaire Under the Oaks," for instance—I would just think, he has big thoughts about that poem. Pages 150 to 180 of Stevens's *Opus Posthumous* contains "Adagia," a compendium of philosophical aphorisms ("To live in the world but outside of existing conceptions of it"), mainly about writing, but on offer are all sorts of aesthetic meditations, really. I found in aggregate it read like a meditation on abstract sorrows. On my fifty-ninth birthday a hardcover journal arrived; it contained thirteen of Jake's drawings inspired by "Adagia"—Jake's note read: *Thirteen ways of looking at Wallace Stevens.*

I scarcely ever voiced an opinion about painting. I only attended one of Jake's classes at Yale, though went on studio visits with him at the Vermont Studio Center and heard perhaps a dozen lectures at galleries, colleges, or private venues. It always struck me that Jake, for all of his self-deprecation, was a born teacher, a nondidactic ("I often wear my heart on my sleeve, but my sleeve might be rolled up"), serious, and highly influential teacher. Among the places he had taught were Cooper Union, Yale University,

University of Pennsylvania, and the School of Visual Arts. In our discussions about teaching, I'd often say that for me, in all honesty, university teaching of creative writing and literature was the next best thing to not teaching, which mainly belied a modicum of ambivalence, along with much gratitude for the employment and being around spirited students; I just never felt that teaching was natural to my character. Whereas Jake often assigned teaching a very high level of regard; for example, he loved singing the praises of his most talented students at Yale; he was devoted to them, and they to him. Anyway, in my case, when it came to knowledge about painting, my experience was that when you know so little, so much proves to be a revelation. Believe me, sitting at his kitchen table, paging through a volume of Ryder, for instance, as Jake offered informal commentary, was a real education. Still, when it had come to that Donald Hall poem, our jousting certitudes made for permanent disagreement. Sure, we heard each other out, but neither of us would budge nor really expected the other to. Oh well, that's how that phone call went that one time.

I guess it was somewhere around 11 p.m. that Jake asked me to make some French toast. Soaking slices of challah in whisked eggs, I said, "In my freshman year at McGill, I was a breakfast cook for a month or two."

"What was the verdict on your cooking?" he asked.

"They made me a waiter."

I served us up the French toast. "I've become a nocturnal soul," Jake said. "I mean, I'm not sleeping much, right?"

"How's the appetite in general?" I said. "You hardly touched the soup before."

"The appetite comes and goes. I get famished, then I can't stomach even the thought of food." He gave the cat a treat. "Hey, remember that Dutch critic—wasn't that what he was? Or art writer of some sort."

I slid in a new cassette. "Now that's what I call a memorable afternoon," I said. As I watched Jake pick at his food, I thought of Chekhov's letter to his fiancée, where he describes how a woman at a dinner he'd been invited to separated her food apart with a fork before each bite, suspiciously examining each piece of fried potato or lamb, to the point that Chekhov thought she ate *forensically*. "I remember how you kicked the Dutch guy out."

"I didn't kick him out," Jake protested. He set aside his plate. "Technically speaking."

"He fled, Jake. He ran for the hills."

"He must've thought I had rabies."

"Yep, *distemper* pretty much describes how you acted toward him. I drove him to the train, remember? The depot over in Hudson. I don't think I ever told you how it went in the car with him."

"I was pissed off, that you paid his ticket to New York."

"Yes, you considered it an apology on your behalf. You were definitely not happy with me."

"You didn't have to *tell* me you paid for his ticket. For some reason you felt the need to tell me."

End of subject of the train ticket.

Jake held up his plate and I took it and set it on the kitchen counter. He hadn't taken a bite.

Thinking back to November of 2006 and the situation with the Dutch art critic, which was not that long after Jake had fallen from a tree while pruning it and had shattered his right wrist, of his painting hand. When word had gotten out, all manner of friends responded. There followed seemingly endless paperwork required to navigate the nightmare medical labyrinth. And most worrisome of all, a sequence of surgeries. I received a lot of woeful updates on the phone. This is all to say that on my visit that included the Dutch writer, Jake was in a lot of pain. (I have a notebook full of sketches of trees he did in this period; in black paint the title reads, *After great pain, a formal feeling comes*, which of course is Emily Dickinson.) I had arrived around noon. A dusting of snow had begun. We had just eaten tuna sandwiches I'd brought when the Dutch critic arrived at the appointed hour (I had no idea he was about to visit), 1 p.m. "Want me to go out to the studio?" I said. But Jake insisted that I should stay right there in the kitchen. I'd intended to visit for a couple of days, so I'd set my old Remington manual typewriter next to my overnight bag in the entranceway to Jake's house. I had an old habit of typing letters wherever I went. Anyway, so instructed, I just sat there in the kitchen, reading in a cursory fashion a few pages of *Daniel Martin*, a novel by John Fowles. But mostly I listened in, which obviously I was meant to do.

Jake introduced me, "This is Howard. He's my butler." I thought that this was an unnecessary private joke; it made me involuntarily collude with his sour predisposition toward his guest. When I walked over to shake hands with him, I saw the Dutch critic write *butler* in English in a small spiral notebook.

His name was Gideon. My best estimate was that he was in his late thirties. He was tall and had a narrow face, longish blond hair with a ponytail fastened by a rubber band. He wore black L.L. Bean snow sneakers, crisply ironed blue jeans, a white shirt under a brown V-neck sweater, a dark green sportscoat with brown patches at the elbows. A very organized look; the one bohemian touch was a stud earring. He had a leather satchel out of which he pulled a compact tape recorder, pen, and a sheath of typed questions. I have forgotten which journal or magazine he worked for, and I might never have known to begin with. He struck me as a little nervous, and the first thing he said, with quite a pronounced accent, was, "Next I go to Los Angeles to interview Mr. R. B. Kitaj. Some people say he's an artist's artist."

"I've always found that a patronizing phrase," Jake said. We were all still standing around in the kitchen. "*Artist's artist.*"

"I am only wondering if a painter such as yourself," Gideon said, "aspires to that level." However he meant this, it was not a good thing to say.

"I have to lie down a while," Jake said. He went into his bedroom and shut the door. *This hasn't started out so well*, I thought.

I was left to make small talk with Gideon. There was a lot of awkward silence. We sat at the kitchen table. Gideon began looking over his notes. At one point he said, "Would you like me to send a postcard informing you whether or not Mr. R. B. Kitaj has also a butler?"

"I imagine he has a studio assistant," I said. "I doubt he has a butler."

"Whatever turns out to be the truth," Gideon said, "I can promise a postcard."

In about half an hour Jake emerged from the bedroom. He sat down on the sofa. "What did you mean by 'a painter such as yourself'?" he said.

Gideon looked stymied. *Oh, boy, this really is not going well*, I thought.

"Do you know this monograph?" Jake said—he located it in a stack of books, catalogues, and monographs on a worktable and held it up for Gideon to see *Kitaj in the Aura of Cézanne and Other Masters.*

"No, I don't know it," Gideon said.

It would have been one thing for Gideon to know or not know the monograph, but quite another to understand that Jake knew it inside-out. In fact, when it was first published in 2001, he read nearly the entire text to me on the phone one night, which took a long time. Neither of us had FAX machines. And keeping with Kitaj, one of the books that Jake voluminously marked up was *Kitaj: Pictures and Conversations*, edited by Julián Ríos. Jake told me that he thought of Kitaj's work as *fearless*. And it was in response to a book of essays about Kitaj written in academically pinched language that Jake had remarked, "To think painting is an intellectual activity is ludicrous," a statement that was eventually used as a caption in an elegant 2008 catalogue of his drawings and paintings of trees and landscapes, at The Betty Cunningham Gallery.

"What did you mean by 'a painter such as yourself'?" Jake said to Gideon. "Did you mean I'm a painter who can appreciate Kitaj's accomplishment?"

"Yes, of course," Gideon said, "that is what I now meant."

"Not everyone feels deeply about Kitaj, but I do," Jake said. "At least about some of his work. Some drawings in particular. The draftsmanship, you could say."

"Good," Gideon said. "I write all of that down."

I was not a stenographer of these couple of hours. But I did enter much of it in a journal, and those entries are far more than paraphrase. It was quite evident that Gideon, intelligent but perhaps a touch obsequious, had done his homework. But I think that the problem was that the questions on his sheet *exclusively* reflected his research of Jake. When Gideon went to use the bathroom, I actually looked at these questions and immediately realized that they weren't questions at all. Copied out and numbered were merely statements made by Jake in interviews quoted in the catalogue of his work at the Rose Art Museum at Brandeis University, May–June 1988. The catalogue itself was sticking out of Gideon's satchel, in clear view.

The catalogue essay had been written by Carl Belz. Within his larger essay, reconditely intimate in tone, Belz had the quotes in darkened print. They served, to some extent, as chronological markers, accompanied by Jake's autobiographical probity and candid self-assessments.

Jake himself gave the essay high marks. "For the time it was written," he had said, "that essay pretty much gets me." However, we never talked all that much about art criticism or art writing in general; Jake often said, "I loathe art-speak"—a general indictment of academic language—which was enough for me. I got the point.

Here are some of the statements that Gideon read aloud that afternoon, following each one with, "Do you still feel this?" or, "Has this thinking been replaced by something else?" or, "Do you actually choose to stick with this?" And Jake outright refused to answer any of those. He'd just shake his head back and forth, and at one point, clearly exasperated, croaked a line from Bob Dylan, "I was so much older then, I'm younger than that now." *Not a bad imitation*, I thought.

> *People want art to come to them and it never will. You have to want to go to art. Investigation, belief, transcendence, everything painting ought to be about. Once you get it together you have a choice, you can work within your established parameters and make the paintings that people come to expect you to make, or you can follow the investigation you're involved in and go where that investigation takes you.*
>
> *Starting around 1962–63, my work was strongly influenced by Milton Resnick. In fact, the paintings were like Resnick clones, but after a few years I felt I hit a dead end; there wasn't any place for my voice to come into them, so at that point I made a complete turn-around. I did some figurative things, some hard-edged paintings, and some modular pieces that I showed downtown with the Park Place group, but it was very unsatisfying—the central involvement with paint was gone, so I just stopped painting for a year, maybe two years.*
>
> *I wanted to get away from the architectural situation involving figure/frame relationships and a dependency on the proportions of the rectangle. I decided to use an oval because*

it seemed to be the most neutral form I could think of. A circle would have more of a symbolic meaning, but I'm not interested in symbol. I'm also not interested in searching for form and developing it through the act of painting. I've always wanted something given, something to observe, something I could watch and build on without having to find it, kind of like someone who paints a still life or a figure, but I was never satisfied painting subjects like that. I also wanted a form that would be known; if I say square, you know what a square is, and if I say oval, you know what an oval is. I felt I could build on that, make the painting something you experience rather than just see.

After dealing with ovals for a couple of years, I suddenly reintroduced a rectangle and a deep space you can get lost in—a turning to, an embrace of that, but at the same time a turning from, a saying good-bye to a place that no longer really existed for me. My painting A Turning To, A Turning From*— it was a sad painting for me to make. I find working now, on one hand, to be incredibly difficult, because I could easily parody them.*

But you have to keep moving, that seems crucial now—not in terms of invention or ideas or systems, but in terms of the language of painting. At this point I'm working on a notion of derailment. The painting will start to move in one direction, and I'll derail it and take it in another direction; when it goes in that direction I'll derail it again, and so on, in order to get it to state its own leads, state what it's about. I try to break the code of the painting and let it take on its own life without any code. That's exciting. I feel I'm painting with an energy and enthusiasm of a 20-year-old, except I have twenty-five years of experience. I've got enough of a history to parody myself, but I'm trying to use those twenty-five years of experience to keep the painting pushed right up against my face—to discover something instead of accepting something I already know.

—Jake Berthot, Rose Art Museum at Brandeis
University, May–June 1988

Now I realize, empathically speaking, that Gideon was in effect translating his every word from Dutch; he thought in Dutch and in his professional life wrote in Dutch; words can make such an arduous journey language to language, and unsuccessfully. Gideon may well have felt that his more original curiosities may not have been accurately represented by his spoken English, but on the other hand he didn't really even try out original curiosities. However, the problem here was not that Gideon read the statements verbatim in English from the Rose Art Museum catalogue. No, the problem was that Gideon's methodology failed to encourage any genuine dialogue. Jake said to him, "We can't get to the truth of anything by just using those old quotes. Can you come up with something else? You've come all the way from Holland."

"I don't think well on my feet, I think the saying goes," Gideon said.

"Do you have any interest in my recent paintings or drawings of trees?"

"I'm ill-prepared for trees, I'm afraid."

"Then that might be a great place to start."

"You fell from a tree, I know this much."

Jake made a rather disingenuous last-ditch effort: "I have some great quotes about trees. How about this, *Those trees are magnificent, but even more magnificent is the sublime and moving space between them, as though with their growth it too increased.* That's from Rilke. My butler here could bring in some recent tree drawings from the studio and we could look at them and talk about that Rilke quote."

"I'm afraid I'm ill-prepared," Gideon said.

I've often tried to really understand what most deeply informed this hopeless stalemate. There are any number of angles at which to view it, some more sympathetic than others. For instance, it may have just all have been bad timing; Jake was in quite a lot of pain, in mortal combat with morphine, as he put it, somewhat exhausted; physical pain so often translated into varietal temperaments. Then there was the fact that Gideon was jet-lagged and had had no caffeine; also, Gideon's hopeful sense of anticipation was so clearly at odds with Jake's prickly reticence. And yet, finally, I'd really have to defer to my friend, who then said, "Don't you have any of your own questions, Gideon? Sure, I meant everything I said back then, everything you quoted I meant and stand by. But don't you have anything you'd like to talk about since say 1988?"

"May I see your studio?" Gideon said.

But that just wasn't going to happen now. "Look," Jake said, "there's pretty much only trees out there. You don't seem much interested in trees. But that's what I'm drawing and painting now. Trees right out my window. Trees."

For all intents and purposes, right there in the kitchen the visit thus ended on the word *trees*. With exaggerated deliberation, almost in slow-motion, Gideon placed his pen, notebook, and sheet of questions into his satchel. "There, I've snapped it closed," he said. "I am out of here. Thank you for a most interesting way to spend time. My respect is unaltered. No need to shake hands. I am departed now. Can your butler take me to my bed and breakfast, please. Of course, I can call a taxi, like how I arrived."

"Oh, come on," Jake said. "How about a cup of coffee?"

"I already didn't get offered a cup of coffee in your house."

"Okay, I understand," Jake said.

"I'll drive Gideon here to his B&B," I said, "then on to the train. I take it you're going to fly out of New York, Gideon, right?"

"Yes," Gideon said. "Tomorrow."

"Okay, then, let's go," I said. "Trains leave from Hudson."

"Thank you," Gideon said. "On the train I can review my notes about Mr. Kitaj." He turned toward Jake. "It was a pleasure to meet a painter such as yourself."

It all reminded me of a Leonard Cohen line, *time flew by but on broken wings*. We were out the door. The dusting had become windblown flurries. In those days I drove a Volvo station wagon. I had new snow tires. I noticed that Gideon had on a very expensive-looking cashmere overcoat. "Does writing about art in Holland make for a pretty good living?" I said, once we were out on the two-lane.

"Maybe better than a butler earns," he said. "My wife is an architect. We combine funds, if that's how to say it." We drove in silence for a while. It may be that his acerbic comment meant he'd figured out that I probably wasn't Jake's butler. Because in his next own question he used the word *friend*. "Did you recognize your friend during our attempt at an interview? Or was it I brought something poisonous out in him?"

I was beginning to enjoy his English. "Poisonous is a little strong, don't you think?" I said.

"I'm just now a little queasy in the emotions," he said.

"I think you need a strong cup of coffee."

"Do you think tea is served at the station?"

"Tea, oh sure, they've got tea."

"I saw your typewriter in the hallway," Gideon said. "It was yours, yes? Do you not use a computer?"

"I've had that typewriter for thirty years," I said. "It was the same one that Bette Davis used."

"Oh, good Lord, that must have cost you a fortune! Or were you family friends with Bette Davis?"

"No, I don't mean Bette Davis's actual former typewriter, Gideon. I mean the same vintage Remington. The same brand of typewriter, Gideon."

"Notice I took a literal meaning," he said.

I have long thought that Heraclitus was right in his elemental platitude, *If friendship is not the air breathed and water needed to drink, call it by another name.* Here, in reprising the whole Gideon incident, a kind of Heraclitean ethics reinstates itself—that friendship demands that your love and fealty should not be compromised just because you are not in your friend's presence. That to whatever extent is humanly possible, you cannot be one kind of friend in person and another kind of friend in absentia. Because your friend has entrusted you with friendship itself, and equivocation of any sort—say, for instance, had I made excuses for or even provided a solacing perspective about Jake's behavior to this Dutch fellow—would have been a form of betrayal. And what is worse, it would have been betrayal out of convenience, just to alleviate a little of the tense and claustrophobic discomfort of riding with Gideon in a car to the train station. So that when I said, "Poisoned is a little strong, don't you think?" I might better have said, "What a schmuck you are!" Angry with myself right then and there in the car, I only wanted to shove Gideon onto the train and get back to Jake's studio and look at drawings of trees.

But, yes, of course I "recognized" my friend Jake in the way he comported himself with the Dutch art critic; it is just that it was none of Gideon's business whether I recognized Jake or not. In fact, I took his question as a violation of propriety. Though I could see he was quite flummoxed, already contending with the fact that he could not possibly, unless by outlandish fabrication, write a professional article about Jake based on his visit. Still, once we approached the ticket counter, I found myself at cross purposes, because I shelled out for the ticket. Gideon snapped the money from my hand and said something I found quite clever, "Thanks for my per diem." And Jake was correct, that in purchasing the ticket, I had inadvertently apologized on his behalf, or some equivalent of that. I waved to the departing train but not to Gideon behind his window.

Back in Accord, when Jake got pissed off at me, I'd said, "Buying him the ticket was generous of me, considering my butler's wages." All was pretty much forgiven right away, I think, almost.

By that time a true blizzard had arrived. I hauled in an armful of wood and set it by the stove. Jake said, "I'd reimburse you, but I know you won't let me."

"You've got that right."

"Hey, with Gideon do you detect any remorse in me? Do you see a sheepish grin? I am so glad that jerk's on the train. Let's go look at some new work, okay?"

Out to the studio we went. It seemed winter had fully arrived. And on that fine, snowy early evening, shattered wrist notwithstanding, my complicated friend Jake was fully human and fully a being.

Back to my final visit at the end of November 2014; when we had finished our recollection about the Dutch art critic, Jake said, "I guess you might someday write about this friendship of ours." That came out of the blue.

"I hadn't thought of doing that," I said. "I mainly wanted to hear your voice later. I mainly wanted to hear us talking. But since you brought it up, what do you think?"

Jake shuffled through some papers again. "I wouldn't mind," he said. "I believe you'd try to get me accurately. But if you screwed it up, then I'd communicate from the dead, right?" He rubbed his hands together and spoke like a demented Bela Lugosi in *Dracula*, "I will somehow express my displeasure. From the other side—heh heh heh."

He continued riffling through some papers and found a quote from Max Frisch. Jake had a German American writer friend who was translating some of Frisch's *Berlin Journal* and had sent Jake some entries. Jake knew that Frisch was one of my most beloved writers. We had watched the film *Voyager* together, which was based on Frisch's novel *Homo Faber*, Jake had loved Sam Shepard's acting, and Julie Delpy's, too. He read the passage:

> To praise a dead man in public and to give a public assurance that you will miss him is the usual expression of our honest mourning in total ignorance of what death is. No face in a coffin has ever told me that the one who has just died misses us. The opposite is all too obvious. So how can I say that my circle of friends among the dead is getting bigger and bigger? The dead man leaves me to the memories of my experiences with him . . . three nights by the Nile, yes, or that final lunch together in the autumnal woods of Pfannenstiel Hill. . . . He, on the other hand, the dead man, has now had an experience without us, the experience that is still to come for me and that cannot be communicated to others—unless that were to happen by a revelation in faith.

"A revelation in faith," Jake said. He closed his eyes, his expression one of chagrin and sadness, and I said, "Jake, what's bothering you?"

"Okay, I guess it's related to that Dutch guy," he said.

"How do you mean?"

And then he said something that took me aback. "I guess I realize what I did with that guy . . . was a refutation of the biographer."

I prepared us each another cup of tea. "Refutation of the biographer," I said.

"Did I use too many big words for you?"

"Ha ha," I said. "Okay, I think I know what you mean by *refutation*. But let me ask you—hypothetically. If somebody was to attempt an actual biography of you—"

"Look, most contemporary painters might get—what? A monograph maybe. A biography—that's completely something else. Very few painters' lives deserve a biography, right?"

"I'm just asking, would you open yourself up to that person?"

"Anyway, they'd really have to hurry, wouldn't they?"

"Fine, if you prefer the past tense—would you *have opened up?*"

"Naw, probably not. But I have the perfect title."

"For what?"

"My biography, which won't ever get written. *I'm a Human but not a Being.*"

"That's just depressing, Jake. I refuse to laugh."

I started to search through a stack of CDs.

"I think what 'revelation in faith' means—partly—is a belief in some sort of afterlife, and some sort of communication between the dead and the living," Jake said. "But I really don't believe in such nonsense. I guess I don't have any expectations, you know? For when I finally die. Just toss my ashes around." We sat for a while not talking. "You know what the French say, when there's a sudden silence at the table?" Jake said. "They say *an angel is passing.*"

"Okay—here's what I expect," I said. "I expect you to under-stand that when you're gone, I'll miss you. Is this strange for you to talk about?"

"It's not morbid, if that's what you mean," he said. "Now and then, given the situation I'm in, I could use a little perspective. But the Dalai Lama doesn't ever pick up the phone. Know what I think? I think it'd be horrible to miss somebody who dies and not be able to tell them—so you do what you just did, tell them when they're still alive. That's the only sure choice you have. But okay, right, end of that subject for now."

Today I was thinking how Jake and I always listened to music. He never failed to have something he wanted me to listen to. I remember the summer after his marriage to his second wife, Kristin, had ended, he was drawing trees while working his way through all of Beethoven's major symphonies. The Fifth and Sixth kept me awake out in the guest room off the studio to all hours one night. When he referred to "my Beethoven trees," I replied, "They don't appear to me more tempestuous than any others of your trees."

"Well, things are going stark raving mad up in the branches," he said.

On that my final visit, I think starting somewhere just after midnight, we listened to a CD I had given Jake in 2012, *The Lost Feuermann: The Japanese Recordings 1934–1936*. Along with Janos Starker (in particular, his recording of Kodaly), Jake's favorite cellist was Emanuel Feuermann. On *The Lost Feuermann* are works by Tchaikowsky, Mendelssohn, Bloch, Godard, Schumann, Shubert, Wrighton, Saint-Saëns, Valentini, Rubenstein, Chopin, and the Japanese composers Taki and Yamada. Jake knew a lot about Feuermann, who made his Vienna debut at age eleven; at age sixteen he was appointed to the faculty of the Gürzenich Conservatory in Cologne and became principal cellist of the Gürzenich Orchestra and a member of the beloved Bram Eldering Quartet. He was forced to leave in 1933 when the Nazis came to power, and during 1934–1935 made his first world tour. In April of 1936, now playing a Stradivarius, his concerts throughout Japan were received with even more glorious reviews than during his previous visit to that country, but paradoxically the audiences were fewer in numbers. A Japanese confidant told Feuermann that while he was still considered the king of cellists, he may have returned too soon to get the reception of a truly honored guest, "Because the Japanese people had already said good-bye to you." Jake had read and marked passages in a biography, *Emanuel Feuermann, Virtuoso*, by Seymour W. Itzkoff.

In my own research, I discovered that *The Lost Feuermann* has come to be something of an anomaly in the Feuermann discography. One critic faulted the recordings as containing "pieces that make for nice encores," yet then wrote, "but of course Feuermann elevates them to high art." But Jake couldn't care less about any of that, he just liked the "antiquarian acoustics" of the live

performances ("Just imagine what was going on in the world then, too—1936"), the scratchiness, the whole somewhat spectral amalgam of static, echoes, audience noises to be heard in the recording. He told me that along with compositions by Erik Satie, it was Feuermann's earlier recordings he almost exclusively listened to while making what he referred to—as did others—as his "red paintings." He felt the cello notes were "received into the paint," an almost theologically lofty assertion, I thought at first, but now having lived for years in the same house with the red painting *Grief for That Past*, I have more understood the phrase, "received into the paint." I've felt it more. The series of five red

42

paintings was exhibited at the Jaffe-Friede and Strauss Galleries at Dartmouth College September 2–29, 1995, and also at The Nielsen Gallery in Boston later the same year. I attended Jake's craft talk at the opening at Dartmouth College and returned to the exhibit two days later with the writer Grace Paley. As Grace looked at each oil on linen painting, she jotted down its title in a notebook. *Squaring Red*, *Evidence*, *Grief for That Past*, *Grief for That Future*, and *Over the Past*. At lunch Grace said, "I read the catalogue and it begins by using that horrible phrase, *painter's painter*. I always hate it when people say of me, she's a writer's writer. But otherwise the catalogue gets how much emotion and anxiety are in the paintings. Plus which, the titles, oy vey, the titles are so . . . what? Well, a person like me gets curious. But, darling, he's your friend, I won't ask anything personal. But *Grief for That Past* and *Over the Past*—tell me, who needs a psychiatrist if you can paint like that?" Well, that was Grace through and through. But I could see that the red paintings had struck deep chords in her.

A few months after the exhibit closed, Jake knew that I had purchased *Grief for That Past*, a 22-inch x 20-inch thickly impastoed red with a white smudged with orange-blue-black column in the center. In a letter he wrote,

> *Erik Satie Erik Satie Erik Satie . . . hours and hours of Erik Satie. . . . Those goddamned Gymnopedies and Gnossiennes and Sarabandes . . . over and over . . . into the red, and that column in the center. . . . I mean, what a person goes through . . . pain . . . the difficult relationships, you get turned inside-out, confusions, not jump-off-a-bridge stuff . . . not really . . . but just ambush after ambush of . . . you get torn up. Those red paintings, I look at them and I remember painting each one. You don't always remember actually the physical connection, but with those, it was different. I remember painting each one. I remember painting. . . . Grief for That*

Past. *Mainly because of that column in the middle, because with that column it's that Rumi thing again. The wound is the place the light enters you. . . . That column's where I wanted the light to enter . . ."*

I slipped *The Lost Feuermann* into the Bose CD player. We listened to Tchaikovsky's "Valse Sentimentale" and Mendelssohn's "Spring Song," and then Jake nodded off on the sofa, but only for the duration of the next three pieces, Bloch's "Prayer," Godard's "Berceuse," and Schumann's "Zigeunerleben." Looking at Jake's expression in repose as he slept brought to mind what Joseph Brodsky had written of Anna Akhmatova, "Asleep, she refused to audition for her death mask; she wasn't ready yet." And I also thought, what does it actually ever mean, when someone reports that their friend died peacefully in his or her sleep? How can anyone really know? It is just a wishful projection, it's what you'd *want* for your friend. I wanted that for Jake.

Just as Schubert's "Serenade" began, Jake startled awake and said as if cursing, "Bad dream," stiffly sat up, took a moment to focus. "Hey, do you think Emma's still angry at me for the Hamlet skull thing?" he said. Of course we can't, perhaps especially in sleep, help where our minds go. Still, I'll forever wonder why Jake suddenly remembered this thing that had occurred twenty years earlier.

It turned out to be the day before Jake met Kristin, during his residency at the Vermont Studio Center in Johnson, Vermont, which ran for two weeks in July of 1994. At the time Jake was living and painting at 105 Bowery in New York. I had picked him up at the train depot outside of Montpelier. The depot seemed right out of Chekhov and in fact in those days was managed by a bulky, good-natured Russian named Vladimir who used to wear plaid shorts, a sweatshirt, and tennis shoes even in winter months. The weather was ghastly, sweeping gusts of rain, literally howling winds half the night. Midnight lightning. Trees fell across our dirt road. The next morning brought a dramatic horizon to the south; five or six dark zeppelin-shaped clouds moved like an armada across a gray sky, out toward New Hampshire. Jane, Emma, Jake, and myself all had oatmeal and toast, and then I drove Jake north to the Vermont Studio Center and what would become a courtship—Jake and Kristin met in the rain on a bridge crossing the Gihon River (of course, the Biblical Gihon is one of four rivers issuing out of the Garden of Eden) and eventually Jake's second marriage. "When he first saw me," Kristin said, "Jake said that I looked like a grasshopper!"

But the evening before, we'd all four sat around in the living room of the farmhouse and watched a faded print of the 1948 film of *Hamlet*; certain frames seemed to have been singed at the edges. Grand figures of the era, the director was Laurence Olivier who also played Prince Hamlet, and Jean Simmons was Ophelia.

The thing to mention here is that one of Jake's signature objects—whenever, rarely, there were recognizable objects in his paintings, that is in his work prior to painting trees—was the skull. For example, as I write this, I'm in my farmhouse looking at *Untitled (Skull)*, a pen and ink on gesso ground on paper, which once was exhibited in the Museum of Modern Art, and which Jake had given to me in 2013.

As *Hamlet* played on the television screen, the adults polished off a bottle of wine. When the famous graveyard scene began—Poor Yorick is exhumed by The First Gravedigger in Act 5, Scene 1; the sight of Yorick's skull evokes a reminiscence by Prince Hamlet—Jake recited the famous lines by heart right along with Olivier. Once finished, Jake said to me, "Hey, why don't we donate our skulls to the Shakespeare festival up in Ontario? That way we'd forever be in Hamlet." To which Emma, age six, stood in pajamas directly in front of Jake and, hands on hips and tearfully glaring, said, "Jake, take that back!" It seemed that Emma didn't mind so much watching an actor hold and speak to a skull, but she didn't like the thought of it being Jake's or my skull. Jake immediately apologized, gave Emma a big hug; stepping back, Emma studied Jake's face, I think to assess if he was or wasn't taking her seriously enough—Jake actually looked quite mortified—and finally appeased, Emma curled up next to him and watched the remainder of the film.

"My guess is, if she even remembers, Emma looks back on it and is glad she was who she was and said what she said," I said. "But come on, Jake, not to worry, she's now twenty-six. She's studied and acted in Shakespeare—a person gains perspective, right?"

"It's weird," he said, "but just now I had a bad dream about it, is the thing."

"About Emma's not forgiving you?"

"No—actually, in the dream, what happened was, our skulls got rejected up in Stratford, Ontario. They chose other skulls."

"Now *that's* funny."

"Hey, there's another slide I want to show you," Jake said. He located it. I held it up to the lamplight. I could barely decipher the tiny print along the white margin: *The Model's Negotiation: David Hockney Meets Elizabeth Taylor*. In terms of materials, hues, and dimensions, it was the same as *When news filtered to the angels, they were overwhelmed by their aloneness*. "I drew this one in 2005," Jake said. In the drawing, the thick dark figure of a very recognizable David Hockney and the equally recognizable Elizabeth Taylor, who looks ever-so-slightly taken aback, lean close to each other, as if in intense conversation. Therefore, the act of negotiation seems very much at work.

"Since it's part of your Artist-Model series," I said, "is it too obvious to say that they're negotiating him wanting to paint her portrait?"

"I mean, I didn't have a specific negotiation in mind, really," Jake said. "More the *act* of negotiation. Maybe the tension of it, or maybe the eroticism of it, or maybe just a kind of bickering, or all of the above. Or none of the above. There's two things. First, I was sitting in a dentist's office looking at some movie magazine of some sort—and there was a photograph of David Hockney standing there talking with Elizabeth Taylor. I knew Hockney hobnobbed in those circles sometimes. So it didn't seem entirely incongruous to me. So there was just the *fact* of them together in the photograph. But that wasn't the most interesting thing for me to think about. I'd been reading some stuff by Stanislavsky. You know, his writing about acting. Somewhere he writes that when two people talk with each other, one wants something from the other one—power or money or sex or something—kind of a cynical idea, but it might've been useful to actors maybe. So right there's the idea of a negotiation. So when I did the Artist-Model drawings I sometimes thought about that."

"I'm so relieved it wasn't just Jake Berthot meets celebrity culture."

"No, but it'd be fair to see it as Berthot *negotiates* with two people he never met, David Hockney and Elizabeth Taylor."

Whenever I now look at the drawing, which is positioned next to *When news filtered to the angels* . . . over the farmhouse piano, I recall writing down something Jake said: "Trees are fixed in time and space, right? But still, on some level, I feel there's a kind of negotiation going on between me and whichever tree. Or me and whichever landscape. Except with landscapes there's two negotiations going on at the same time—just to stay with that idea. There's the one between me and the landscape itself. Then there's the one between me and Cézanne. Cézanne's never not there. I just had to get used to that."

During Yamada's "Karatachi no Hana," Jake nodded off yet again. For no logical reason, I felt that he was going to sleep a while. I decided to go out to the studio. When I switched on the lights, I saw an in-progress canvas, a skull coming into view, which

leaned against the far wall. Two drawings of trees were in progress on a wide worktable. Also, on the table was a square package wrapped in brown butcher paper. I wondered how long it had really been since Jake was last in the studio, I think five months or more. Printed in black Magic Marker on the butcher paper was FOR HOWARD. In pencil in scrawled cursive was, *Friendship can offer what the world cannot—forgiveness, love, friendship itself.* The quote was attributed to Heraclitus.

For some unaccountable reason I didn't unwrap the package until a month after Jake died. Inside were two tree drawings, including *Study for River Maple.*

CHAPTER 4

WRITING
ON DRAWINGS

S omewhere around 1 a.m., give or take half an hour, with *The Lost Feuermann* playing for the second time ("When I go to the concert hall," André Gide wrote, "I am listening for music to accompany life, and the end of life. Even if I have heard a piece of music a hundred times, I must try to experience it without nostalgia as much as a sense of possibility"). Jake said, "On the bed out in the studio is a box of drawings. Bring them in here, will you."

In the storeroom between studio and guest room, I had seen many such flat boxes, each full of drawings. Having gone out and retrieved the box, I set it on the kitchen table and Jake, a slight whistle in his breathing, shuffled over and sat at the table. He opened the box and we went through them one by one. They were each 11 inches x 18 inches and each had a different "text" on it. I remembered this group and in fact remembered the exact date I'd first seen them, 10/10/2010, not for any occult implication of the sequence, not at all, but because it was the first time Jake had wanted to record conversations. And he must have, at that moment, seen a look of surprise, if not incredulity, cross my face; the paradox that registered was, *such a private man wants to record conversations.* Well, he must have put a lot of thought into it. "This machine," he said. "—I'm thinking of doing some personal writing sometime. Not sure what kind yet. Do you mind? Not that I'll say anything worth keeping. But my memory's got more holes in it than before." Therefore, in the blink of an eye, began four subsequent years of intermittent recording. He always made duplicates for me, and each would arrive in a padded mailer, along with a handwritten letter on yellow legal pad paper. I should mention, too, that the week before Jake died, he said on the phone, "Did you keep all those tapes?" When I said, "Of course," he said, "Good, because I didn't." I never knew if this meant that all along he had sent me the originals, or that he had decided to toss his copies out, or what. Yet another thing I'd never know.

Tapping his fingers on the stack of drawings, he said, "Take these home with you, okay?" It was an overwhelming gift, and yet all I could do in response was just nod in the affirmative. Because I knew from experience that if I had said, "This is too much," he'd most likely say, "Did you consider the fact that I gave this a lot of thought?"

Thinking back to 10/10/2010, on that crisp clear autumn afternoon, we had driven to Hudson, New York, to visit the Turkish-born photographer Sedat Pakay and look at his archive of black-and-white photographs that he had taken in the 1960s and 1970s of James Baldwin in Istanbul, where Baldwin had written some of his most important essays, and in Hollywood, where he was working on a screenplay about Malcom X. We stayed for four hours and viewed 156 photographs. Sedat's running commentary and detailed anecdotes made for a generous portrait of his and Baldwin's long friendship. On the drive back to Accord, Jake said, "I've got some drawings I want to show you. And I've got a new remix of *Blonde on Blonde* special ordered. It's got some rare outtakes, plus a booklet full of fun Dylan facts and photographs. You heard it yet?"

"No," I said.

"I'll play it for you."

Back in Accord, Jake seemed in relatively good spirits. After I'd set up in the guest room and walked into the house, he said, "I'm making vegetarian chili. Living alone, I cook with leftovers in mind." I saw the big black pot on the stove. "It's been a pretty good week. My cat came back after two nights in the wilderness, and I've been in the studio every day and half the night. Plus, the *Blonde on Blonde* remix and now this visit to Sedat and seeing all those amazing photographs. Let's see, what else? Oh, yeah, pain meds for my back haven't been making me zany, but that comes and goes. I don't know. Some days you barely get through, others you really live."

We had dinner on the back porch, wearing our sweaters and jackets, no breeze to speak of, still warm enough to do that. Early stars seen through the trees. We each had a glass of whiskey, then went out to the studio where Jake showed me a new painting, *The Longing For*, that consisted of the long, slim trunk of a tree, probably a birch, which seemed to be imploring upward; the canvas was thickly cloaked in dark greens, with reprieves of smudged white on the left and upper right, and all of it to my mind made for a work of penetrating melancholy.

In the studio, then, was when Jake first showed me the eleven drawings that I now have in my Vermont farmhouse. As we looked at them, I noticed that they had been composed between 1984 and 1986. The first one was titled *In the middle of the night*, and it certainly had a kind of frenetic wakefulness that befit its title.

On the upper section of each of the drawings were various pen-and-ink Milky Way eddies, ghostly presences, angels, symbolic bric-a-brac, scribbles, flocks of sombrero-shapes. On the lower section of each drawing was a "text"—that is, Jake's often encoded cursive writing, stylized or torqued into obscurity, you might say. On drawing after drawing, this writing was, of course, a considered part of the overall composition. And yet to me these "texts" invited a separate curiosity—after all, wasn't it natural to want to know what the artist had actually written? Indeed most of the writing was indecipherable, which suggested that it functioned as writing Jake wanted to exist, in fact, to incorrigibly resist being read. I came to consider it as words drawn up from Jake's calligraphic inner life, but I still wanted to read that inner life.

As if preempting my asking what the writing actually said—and I might have asked that very thing—Jake said, "Drawings aren't meant to be read but wholly taken in."

"Nice platitude," I said. "Just as a first impression, I can make out about 80 percent of the writing on these drawings."

Jake laughed a little. "Nobody asked you to be a Benedictine monk," he said.

"Oh, you really like that image, don't you? Robed man hunched over a copy table. In the Abbey of Cluny. *Habitare recum.*"

"I didn't take Latin. What's that mean?"

"*To dwell with the self.*"

"Now, that's the biggest challenge of all, right."

"Was some of this writing on your drawings ever anything else to begin with, or was it all just sort of stream of consciousness, or what?"

"Let me go get something." He disappeared into the studio for a few moments and then returned with a few hardbound journals. I sat on the Eames chair paging through them as Jake made two espressos and brought those along with slices of coffee cake in on a tray. "Those journals contain some of the original stuff," he said.

As I soon discovered, by "original" he literally meant stanzas of poetry and passages of prose he had copied out in the journals, some of which he eventually had transferred to drawings. But he also meant writing that had sprung whole cloth, as it were, from his imagination. Many of those read something like surrealist prose-poems, hyperbolically associational, resembling the style of

Paul Éluard, say, or Rene Arnholst, or perhaps one of Emmeline Archambault's so-called "anxious confessions."

Here is an example of one of Jake's "original" compositions which is on one of the eleven drawings under discussion here.

> *For the life of me dawn and dusk similar light-wise but dissimilar emotion-wise Ryder I'll write a letter to Ryder he'll clarify all this hyphen hyphen hyphen today is March 19, 1817 no it isn't it's March 19, 1979 like they say any date that begins with March is a complete sentence march fourth march twentieth let's see what Cezanne has to say about something anything. Really my feeling is my own ineptitude at love or love's ineptitude at drawing me out how about a séance wherein true love is summoned forth therefore I can kick everyone else out of the room and have love to myself at least till the candles burn all the way down orb and Venus on the Half-Shell the way the ocean surf is so loud you think you are losing your hearing 186649 I can recall my first phone number as a child but none after not even presently, my father was a sea gull wave good-bye I'm off to the garbage dump near Niagara Falls but you stay busy read a comic book I'm off with the other gulls be resourceful "Comedy of Errors" all the day's heartbeats have errata my father put a postscript emotion at breakfast what a way to start the day cereal cheerios with a sea gull, I spent today sharpening pencils and wearing them to a nub every day of my life is like this if the lights blink out just draw in the dark 19/March 1979.*

Today, January 25, 2022, at my farmhouse's kitchen table I have been looking at the eleven drawings with writing on them, and finally figured out which two quotes in Jake's journals were transferred to separate drawings, but Jake made sure they were, in this second incarnation, not completely readable. There are twelve sentences from "Letters to Benvenuta" by Rilke, and there are eighteen sentences from a travelogue in volume 2 of George Eliot's *Life and Letters*. On a third drawing, Jake had adjoined two consecutive pages, in the original German, from Kafka's *Letter to the Father*. I don't read German, but I could see that Jake had not obscured the letters; that is, someone who read German could fully understand Kafka's writing. "*Letter to the Father* is one of my favorite books," Jake said. "But back in the day, once I started serious therapy, it was too painful to read again. Even now—looking at that drawing with the Kafka on it— just reminds me of how painful those therapy sessions were, talking about my own dad. The break-up of my parents' marriage and all of that stuff. Jesus, let alone the fact that I ended up shacking up with my therapist for a while. Talk about one of Dante's hells! What was I thinking?"

I want to meditate on something here for a moment. One of the conclusions I arrived at about our friendship is that Jake wanted me to know, in so many words, that he abhorred the notion of anyone thinking of him as some paradigm of the processual—that is, he didn't see himself as an artist whose personal life and his painting should be too readily seen as intertwined. He'd put this directly, "My work is not autobiographical—it's that painting lets me get at emotions that the rest of life doesn't. So I like to keep painting and life separate in that sense."

So, for instance, while sitting around, speaking in an unguarded mood, he'd reveal with specificity the source griefs that, in the red paintings, had led to titles such as *Grief for That Past*, or *Grief Remembered*. Yet in interviews about the red paintings, he was at best opaque, and sometimes he'd just shut down. On occasion, when an interlocuter got too close to the heart of the matter, Jake would briefly pontificate on emotion in art.

"The deepest beauty in art is mysterious," he once said to me, "and all else is useless commentary." I slightly called him out on that. "Well, maybe in the right hands," I said, "commentary might capture the mysteriousness, or at least try to describe it."

"Language can't do any of that," he said.

End of subject. I didn't say any more, mainly because it was the most peaceful option. But the thing was, Jake had an original mind and most of the time I really loved how it worked. Besides, what other response did I expect from my friend who could be so well defended, but who also had said, "Painting saves me. I've mainly fucked up every other part of my life, except maybe a few friendships and maybe my teaching. Don't ask me to describe my nature. But I can feel my nature at work when I'm painting. That's enough to ask, I think."

What to make, then, of all this writing on drawings. Every day in my farmhouse I walk past their indecipherable texts. Yet in the end, the question for me is not what all of the writing actually says, but how did literature open the drawings up. And what do I mean by "open the drawings up" anyway? Well, since four of the eleven drawings have the same quote from Emily Dickinson—*after great pain, a formal feeling comes*—very clearly written, Jake was declaring, pure and simple, their indispensability to his life and work, and that simple fact should be enough for me. "It just feels powerfully intimate, to put those words there," he said. "I thought it out, I thought it out. There were lots of literary quotes I wanted to put on drawings, but I couldn't do the right kind of drawing to fit them together."

"But that Dickinson line just keeps showing up, doesn't it?" I said, promoting the obvious as a revelation, I suppose.

"Yeah, it would take me a whole other lifetime to figure out why," he said. "—it's so haunting and beautiful. Maybe I more mean, it'd take me a thousand drawings with the Dickinson on them to help me figure it out. I don't know. What I do know is, there's probably nothing great poetry can't do for a person like me. So, as an artist, I was just trying to figure out what it could do for my drawings."

It sometimes really gobsmacks me to think about how *after great pain, a formal feeling comes* reverberated through Jake's life, and at so many difficult moments seemed to serve as an indispensable source of introspection for him. When his and Kristin's marriage broke up, he said, "How Dickinson applies is kind of literal, I guess you could say. You have this unbearable pain. Some time passes. You gain a little composure. Maybe not a lot, but some. Maybe Helen Vendler would have a field day with all that subjectivity, huh? Maybe I should read her on Dickinson. But you know how I think, right? Reading Vendler might take something away from how I've come to coexist with Emily Dickinson—*after great pain* kind of already lives inside me."

There was really nothing I could say to that.

CHAPTER 5

WOMAN SHOUTING IN THE CEMETERY ON A RAINY DAY

"Would you mind heating up some of that soup?" Jake said. "I'm going to try to eat something." I got out the bowls of potato-leek I'd put in the refrigerator, emptied them into a small pot, and heated them on the stove for a few minutes. Jake wasn't about to move from the sofa, so I set a bowl of soup on the table in front of him. "How about some Chet Baker?" he said.

I scoured the CDs stacked here and there and found CHET BAKER 1, which had a rendition of "Big Deal on Madonna Street." Jake's favorite cut. The whole thing was signature Chet Baker, noir trumpet, drummer's whispering brush work, the lilt and drift of Baker's too-cool-for-school voice. A total hep cat deity. As soothing Chet Baker drifted out into the room, Jake was sipping the soup—that was a nice thing—and trying to recall where he'd left a particular notebook. Finally, he said, "I think it's on a shelf in the guest room out in the studio."

"What's in it?" I said.

"I think on the first page is that woman in the cemetery drawing—I think so at least. There's five or six black notebooks—it's one of those."

"Oh my God, I almost completely forgot about her! Her yelling at the gravestone."

"If it's not on the bookshelf, check the wooden trunk by the bed."

I headed out to the studio, but on my way, I noticed, on a shelf next to some art books and *Collected Poems of Frank O'Hara*, a yellow legal pad. I recognized Jake's handwriting and that he'd been composing a letter. Most of Jake's letters that survived all the changes of address, packing and unpacking of trunks and boxes, misplacement of files, but also just the way a letter, perhaps tucked into a book, surfaces years after you thought it lost, were with few exceptions written on yellow legal pads. As for this particular letter, I saw that it was addressed to me, so I took it out to the studio. It was dated November 26, the day before my final visit: "*I'm sorry to have canceled . . . but let's talk on the phone,*" it began. Clearly Jake had thought he wasn't going to be up to my visit. Like he had said, he'd been cancelling a lot of appointments of late. The letter continued,

> *I'm not working on a skull . . . still can't get to the studio . . . but I was working on one . . . months ago. . . . I had two drawings of skulls too—not a return but continuation . . . one of my patterns. . . . Away from skulls for years, then back to them . . . away, back . . . and I can only say . . . it's as if I'm looking* DEATH *(skulls) straight in the face. . . . I feel the painting and drawings (skulls) . . . have reached deeper than I have ever looked and gone before . . . they're not macabre . . . but they are totally . . . one on hand, in presence/gaze . . . etc etc etc . . . I feel each one . . . in similar ways, are . . . that I've been working with the "idea" . . . not just in aesthetic terms but literally about perpetual* TIME *. . . looking right at things . . . right at "the life" of the skull . . . which doesn't . . .*

not to me . . . in or out of the studio . . . in or out of this Hell
cancer and non-being . . . doesn't seem contradictory . . .

Those ellipses: every single one of Jake's handwritten letters contained many ellipses, and I finally came to believe they served the individual sentences they resided in in the way Stravinsky (in conversation with Robert Craft) spoke of "the silence between notes is where the music takes a moment to breathe, readies itself for the next commitment to the whole composition. Silence contains anticipation—what is to come next? Silence with compositional purpose."

In the studio, I found the sketchbook; back in the house, I returned the legal pad to where I'd found it. I feel that I should mention here that a few days after my final visit with Jake, I received this very same letter—he'd simply decided to continue it, and I was particularly grateful he hadn't felt the need to cross out the "I'm sorry to have canceled" part; I thought that was honest and funny. Anyway, here is the remainder of the letter:

> *. . . I sit here . . . or I'm in bed trying to read. . . . And I close my*
> *eyes and see those skulls . . . out in the studio . . . you know? . . .*
> *life of the skulls unfinished because I'm not a BEING. . . .*
> *I'm HUMAN because I'm "seeing" them, but I can't get out to*
> *them . . . not a BEING.*
>
> *I mean, Howard, I'm striving to keep THINKING . . . !!!!*
> *TO KEEP THINKING . . .*
> *STRIVING TO KEEP THINKING AND KEEP DAY*
> *DREAMING AND NIGHT DREAMING*
>
> *Love, Jake*

In from the studio, I sat next to Jake on the sofa, set the notebook down on the table. It contained a hodgepodge of loose papers: sketches, museum and gallery correspondences, postcards.

When he found four sheets of 8-by-10-inch paper, he said, "Ah, I'll be goddamned, here she is!" On those sheets were perhaps twenty separate pencil sketches of a woman kneeling in front of a gravestone.

Seeing these kneeling women took us back to that July morning in 1994, when I had driven Jake to his residency at the Vermont Studio Center. It was raining cats and dogs. When we stopped at the Hardwick diner for a coffee, Jake said, "I don't have to be at VSC until dinner, really. You know how everyone sits together in the communal dining room. I have my craft talk tonight, too. I'll show some slides."

"I'm staying for that," I said.

"Do you want to drive around a little more this afternoon, though?" Jake said. "It's only two o'clock or so. I just want to look at the landscape, maybe let's drive north for a while."

"Let's go up to Craftsbury Common," I said. "There's a great general store. There's a small private college, Sterling College, know what their motto is? *Working Hands—Working Minds.* It's a very nice village."

"I take it there's a common."

"Quite a big grassy common, and some old houses on the common. I've always felt peaceful there. For whatever reasons, peaceful."

"Let's drive up there."

The windshield wipers clacking away, we drove through the long stretch of rolling farmland, with grand vistas in every direction, even in the rain. In thirty or so minutes, we got to Craftsbury. We passed the somewhat Amish-looking aggregate of white wooden buildings that comprised Sterling College, and then I slowed the car down as we drove past the cemetery located at the southeast edge of Craftsbury Common since 1798. A nineteenth-century

Vermont governor and US senator, Samuel Crafts, is buried there.

"Hey—look!" Jake said, rapping his window with his knuckles, and then rolling down the window. "What's she—?" I stopped the car and looked over to where Jake had indicated. Rain blew in. "Look at that—" he said.

Three or four rows of gravestones into the cemetery, a woman of indeterminate age was on her knees in front of a gravestone. The gravestone looked of average size, weatherworn granite, rounded at the top, commonplace. The woman was dressed in a black rain slicker, and on her head was a yellow sou'wester hat so bright that it almost seemed illuminated from within. Underneath the slicker she had on a black sweatshirt, its hood partially hiding her face. She wore old-school buckled galoshes. Even through the rain, we could hear that she was shouting and sobbing herself hoarse. At the same time, she tore out page after page from a dark-covered book, and the pages flew every which way in the rainy wind, fluttering and landing all over the closest precinct of the cemetery, like the confetti of untenable anger, grief, and who knows what else. At one point she pressed her forehead against the gravestone, then suddenly recoiled and tore out more pages. "What do you think we're seeing here?" Jake said. It was dramatic and upsetting and, the woman engrossed in her cacophonous distress, we couldn't look away.

"I have no idea," I said.

Her shouting was mostly unintelligible, though a few fragments could be deciphered. "Goddamn you!" and "should have told," but complete sentences, if she could've even managed one while in such high dudgeon, were lost in the rainy gusts and rain brailling the puddles of the road, and plunking off the hood of the car and so on. She tore out page after page, and finally threw the book as far as she could from her kneeling position. We saw it ricochet off a gravestone. Her voice then became more a guttural howl, just for a brief moment. Then she sat down legs crossed, then clutched her legs, rocking back and forth. "Should we see if she needs some help or something?" I said. "Maybe it's none of our business," Jake said. In a few minutes she got to her feet, stood stiffly, arms flat against her body, turned and stared at our car. Jake remained in the front seat, but I got out and leaned against the trunk of the car.

She simply kept staring. A page of the book clung to her shoulder. She stared and stared. I felt properly caught out and indicted. Then she pulled down the hood of her sweatshirt and we could see that she had white-gray hair and was perhaps seventy, quite possibly older. Now an odd thing in the rain, she reached into the inside pocket of her slicker, took out a pack of cigarettes and a lighter, lit a cigarette, and took a few puffs, all the while cupping her left hand over the cigarette so the rain wouldn't douse it, and she never took her eyes off us.

"Definitely time to leave," Jake said when I got back behind the wheel. We slowly drove north out of Craftsbury Common. I glimpsed the woman in the rearview mirror as she walked from the cemetery. Jake took out a small sketchbook and a pen from his satchel and sketched something, and we didn't say a word for a while. We drove up near to the Canadian border. We stopped at the charred ruins of a duckpin bowling alley, which was not really located in any village; it had been part red brick and part wood, and I told Jake that its three alleys were said to have actually crossed the US-Canada border. Built in 1940, it had closed in 1965. I had at one point found a postcard photograph of it in a thrift shop in St. Johnsbury: three women bowlers stood holding small American flags and behind them, in clear view, two pin boys and a pin girl held small Canadian flags in front of ten upright duckpins. At one point, I told Jake, I had researched this bowling alley, thinking of putting it into a short story—nothing finally came of this, but I'd had in mind illicit love letters exported and imported inside bowling balls, a Canadian American epistolary love affair between two wives of those citizenships. I sort of regaled Jake about all of this. From the ruins we drove south. We listened to some classical music on the radio; we talked about Jake's present loneliness, his desire to meet someone, to fall in love. "I mean, there's no violins playing or anything like that," he said, "but I'm feeling pessimistic about all of that, you know?" When we arrived to Craftsbury Common again, Jake said somewhat insistently, "Let's go see what book it was she tore up." I stopped the car along the common, and each of us holding an umbrella, we walked across the road and into the cemetery.

"Alas, poor Yorick," Jake said.

"Look, Jake, I actually thought your idea about donating our skulls to the Shakespeare festival up in Ontario was a great idea. We'd have to arrange it in our wills or something."

"Emma wouldn't abide by that."

"That's probably true."

"You and Jane are truly blessed, you know? With that daughter of yours. Such a strong personality. Such an amazing spirit. But yeah, I'm still in favor of the idea."

Almost right away we saw pages on the ground; several were pasted by rain and wind to gravestones. "I see the book!" Jake said, starting toward it. But on his way he peeled a page from a gravestone, squinted down at it, then half-shouted out loud, "'Then a spirit lifted me up, and brought me unto the east gate of the Lord's house, which looketh eastward; and behold at the door of the gate five and twenty men; and I saw in the midst of them Jaazaniah the son of Azzur, and Pelathiah the son of Benaiahj, princess of the people. . . .' I can't pronounce these names . . ."

"What book of the Bible is that from, do you think?" I said, walking over.

"Top of the page says Ezekiel," Jake said.

Jake leaned over and picked up another page. "This page is from Proverbs: 'Wisdom crieth aloud in the street, she uttereth her voice in the broad places; she calleth at the head of the noisy streets, all the entrances of the gates, in the city, she uttereth her words, "How long, ye thoughtless, will ye lodge thoughtlessness? And how long will scorners delight them in scorning, and fools hate knowledge?"' I'd like an answer to that myself," Jake said.

Jake picked up the tattered and torn Bible and slipped it into his jacket pocket. "Talk about a person having righteous anger," he said. "I mean, that woman! Do you remember which gravestone she was shouting at?"

"Somewhere over there," I said, sweeping my arm to take in five or six stones. I read the names above a few of the epitaphs.

Jake said, "Any of them die recently?"

"Well, this one guy about fifty years ago."

"Could be her father, maybe." Jake held up the Bible for me to see. "She tore half the pages out."

I took the Bible and looked on the inside cover, in case there was a name inscribed. No luck there. I handed it back to Jake.

"I'm soaked through," he said.

"Let's go."

South to Hardwick, then from Hardwick we drove west on Route 15 and in about forty minutes reached Johnson, turned right off the main drag and pulled into the gravel lot in front of the two-story house whose four apartments were reserved for visiting faculty. The rain had let up a little. Just as we stepped from the car, John Gregg, an inveterate Ancient Mariner type (Jake had little patience with him) and yet to everyone's perpetual benefit, one of the founders of VSC in 1984, called out "Jake!" and walked right over. Jake introduced me and the three of us went into the guest house. John showed Jake his room, handed him a folder of faculty materials along with keys to the room and house, and said, "See you at dinner." "He didn't invite you," Jake said, "but you're invited." Jake set some shirts, trousers, and socks in two dresser drawers, set his shaving kit in the bathroom and his brown leather suitcase in a corner, and we walked over to the dining hall. Soon about forty painters and writers of all ages meandered in, filled plates from the cafeteria-style bins of food, and distributed themselves at different tables, already buzzing with conversation. Four painters sat at our table, then John sat with us, and immediately said to no one in particular, "I've been thinking about my childhood—"; Jake had officially begun his residency.

After dinner there was an hour break. I noticed that it had finally stopped raining. Jake and I walked over to the porch of the guest house and sat on a sofa and chair and talked awhile. Jake went in to get his slides. Just before 7:30 p.m., we walked back to the dining hall, where a screen and slide projector had been set up. John introduced Jake rather obtusely, saying absolutely nothing about his work. "You'll notice this evening we have a full house. Yes, our craft talks are open to the public. And we got a lot of calls about Jake Berthot being here." That was pretty much it.

In his talk, Jake basically riffed from notes, but he began somewhat formally, or as formally as I'd ever heard him:

"In reading Camus, I came across something that seemed to apply to my painting. Camus writes, 'I cannot tolerate in a person convenient spiritual surfaces.' He was responding to a man who seemed to lack any originality in his philosophy of life—that is, he took a little Buddhism from here, a little Zoroastrianism from there, a little Kabbalah, a little Christian monasticism—and for Camus, this completely lacked gravitas, or real meaning, let alone any attempt at original thinking. Now, of course, he was talking about a person and not about painting. But I immediately thought, this can apply to thinking about a painting life. Or at least my own painting life. I thought a lot about 'convenient surfaces.' Which might be the same as saying you're not going deep enough into your work. And relying too much on connecting with what's popular, or what's a trend, all of what's so wrong and limiting in the contemporary world of art . . . because you have to keep questioning the sociolect—that's a word I got from reading someone, I can't remember who—the convenient painterly discourses of your own generation. I myself for a long time dealt with convenient surfaces—just to keep using that phrase. [He showed a slide of a painting by Milton Resnick.] I mean, here's a painting by my mentor, Milton Resnick—and [next slide] now here's a painting I did under the complete and happy and grateful and everything else *influence* of Milton's work. Which was always a real gift to me. And still is. But after a while, I realized that I was so absorbed in Milton's paintings, I couldn't—as poets like to say— find my own voice. That might sound simple and obvious, but it wasn't. Actually, it was so complicated that I stopped painting for a while. Like Robert Frost said, the only way out is through. I had to break through the convenient surfaces . . . though I always struggled with . . . surfaces . . . with Milton's influence . . . because I could never capture the deepest elements of Milton's work . . . the deepest language in the paint itself. What it held to the light, what it kept from the light. The paint itself. So these slides I'm going to show now cover about twenty-five years of my work. It's been one continual attempt to deepen things in the work. To keep evolving. To stay alert . . . to not getting lazy . . . or of worrying what anyone might think. To just go deeper."

I can't honestly say that Jake's bridging Camus' "spiritual surfaces" to his own painting was all that successful, but the painters in the audience, from the expressions on their faces, were all in. They really got it. They got Jake's roundabout style of lecturing. And that's all that really mattered.

Jake's presentation lasted about an hour. During the Q&A, a woman sitting toward the back, with a scratchy voice, said, "Do you consider painting a way to deal with emotions—such as anger? I just mean, are you ever surprised by what emotions occur when you are working on a painting?" I turned to see who had asked this question and was absolutely stunned to see—and definitely recognize—the woman from the cemetery. I looked at Jake, who was now looking at me, slowly shaking his head back and forth, incredulous. All I could think was, *Jake's jacket is draped over the chair next to him and in the pocket is this woman's Bible.* Jake completely maintained his composure, though I could tell he was slightly unnerved. "Well, painting and emotions," he said and then more or less stumbled through a half-baked answer, " . . . for instance, those red paintings in the slides? They had a lot of emotion in them, as far as I'm concerned." Then he abruptly stopped. There followed at least ten more questions, evidence of a rapt and inquisitive audience; no dud questions, really. Finally, John Gregg stood and said, "Okay, I think we've made Mr. Berthot work hard enough for tonight." There was applause and most of the painters, writers, and outside guests scattered out into the night, though a few lingered at tables to talk. There was coffee available all night, from a big, insulated silver-tone dispenser near the kitchen area.

I accompanied Jake back to the guest house porch. "Nice craft talk," I said.

"It's not that comfortable for me," he said. "Teaching's one thing—autobiographical stuff is something else"

"I think people got what you were saying. I'd like to read it—I saw the first part was typed out."

"Glutton for punishment," he said, handing me the pages. "Keep that. I made a copy." He went inside and brought out a bottle of Scotch and two glasses. "I've got a long drive," I said, "so maybe just a sip. I'll get coffee later. "We clinked glasses and suddenly Jake leaned forward, grasped my wrist, and said, "Jesus wept!—you *saw* her, right? We have to talk about this!"

"Of course I saw her. She stood up to ask her question, Jake."

"I mean, that definitely was her, right?"

"It definitely was."

"I'm going to ask John Gregg if he knows her," Jake said. "How often she comes to lectures. I'm going to ask him."

"Do you think she recognized you—or even me?"

"I couldn't really tell. I mean, you were right there. She asked her question. She sat listening to my answer, such as it was. I was flabbergasted. I was looking right at her. I saw absolutely no signs of recognition, though. None. She just nodded and smiled and said thank you, right? What is her life? *Unfuckingbelievable!*"

"This very afternoon, she's screaming in the rain," I said. "In a cemetery. Next thing on her agenda is, what? Maybe have a quiet dinner, then attend a craft talk by a visiting painter. Go figure."

"Well, you tend to think in narratives," Jake said.

We sat awhile. I don't recall what we talked about. But at one point, we looked over and saw, silhouetted beneath ceiling lights misted by moisture in the air, a figure standing on the railed porch outside the dining hall. She bent slightly, lit a cigarette, and even out of the rain, cupped her hand over the cigarette as she lifted it to her mouth. The gesture was all déjà vu. She looked over at the guest house porch, but then a few others stepped out of the main building, laughing and talking, and she moved right along. "That has to be her," I said.

"Same galoshes," Jake said. "Definitely the same galoshes."

Two nights later at about eleven o'clock, the phone rang in my farmhouse and, when I said hello, right away I could hear that Jake was full of enthusiasm, and as it turned out, on three counts. First, he'd had "very productive" studio visits with some of the resident painters. Second, "I found out a few things about our woman in question," he said. "She's—are you sitting down? She's a retired or semi-retired psychoanalyst. At least according to Mr. Gregg. What we witnessed was a shrink screaming at a gravestone and tearing a Bible to shreds."

"Now that's got to be a once-in-a-lifetime thing," I said.

"But also, she herself has been a writer here at VSC. Working on a memoir of some sort. Again, that's the Gospel According to John—Gregg. He knew right away who I was describing. I didn't tell him about the cemetery, though."

"Well, there's no reason anybody—shrink or no shrink—can't express . . ."

"So that's what you're calling it, *expression?* I mean, yeah, she was expressing all right."

"Maybe she goes to the cemetery to yell and scream all the time, Jake. Maybe she goes through a Bible per week. How the fuck should I know? By the way, I'm very happy to say you sound in good spirits."

Here came the third reason. ". . . because also also also, my friend—I've met, just walking across a bridge, I met an absolutely *charming*, amazing woman, Kristin. She's a painter here. I'm over the moon."

"I just now closed my eyes and saw loneliness fly out your window."

Intermittently for about three years after the cemetery incident, in the margins of letters or on separate pieces of manila paper, were sketches of the mystery therapist in various postures, always in front of a gravestone. Some depict Bible pages fluttering in the air. Some depict slants of rain. A few depict angels hovering over the cemetery. And one has a voice balloon over the woman's head; inside the balloon it reads PROVERBS–EZEKIEL–FREUD!!!! SHOULD HAVE TOLD YOU . . .

I want to stay with Jake's letters a little while longer here. Because our friendship was, as much as anything, an epistolary relationship; over decades one builds a tradition of exchanging letters, and that tradition dictated (as *in accordance to the dictates of your conscience*) that if Jake wrote a letter, he expected one back. I guess I felt the same way. In this regard, letter writing had its own ethical insistences. I have a number of Jake's letters which include sentences such as "I wrote . . . weeks ago . . . didn't hear back . . . hope all is okay," or with equivalent queries and concerns, and an understated hint of admonishment, "I guess reliance can lead to sensitivities," if I was delinquent in posting a letter after more than a month after receiving one. But what was definitely true, during any considerably long time (sometimes a year or even more) when we did not see each other, letters were what Katherine Mansfield thought they should be, "an integral part of the mandate of absence." If Jake sent me a book to read, I read it and we would discuss it. In a letter dated November 8, 2009, Jake wrote:

> *Dear Howard . . . okay . . . Now let me address the Coetzee novel you sent. . . . There's an UNCOMPROMISED and UNCOMPROMISING writer . . . severe . . . but also . . . the prose . . . gets hypnotic . . . I tore right through Disgrace . . . (that one kept me up at night) . . . but then . . . I was back in the studio long hours . . . so I set aside Elizabeth Costello. . . . I know you admire it . . . and haven't got back to it yet . . . Let's talk about Coetzee . . . in a way there's no one I'd rather be reading now . . . but definitely have to divvy him out . . . you know? I mean, it's like you wake up and your heart is a South African parched landscape . . .*
>
> *Maybe with strange spiky flowers out in the middle of NOWHERE . . . kind of the opposite, in a way . . . in a way the opposite of my close trees here and Ryder landscapes . . .*
>
> *Etc etc etc . . . terrible and redemptive human behaviors in Coetzee . . . anyway . . . DISGRACE . . . if you bring the DVD of the film we can watch it together . . . in some ways I think Malkovich is the most DISTURBING presence on screen . . . !!!*

I would have to say that the book that engendered—in fact over the length of five letters—the longest deliberation was *Mark Rothko*, the biography by James. E. Breslin. It was originally published in 1993 and Jake may have read it first thing back then, but from his letters and from several conversations I got the distinct impression that he at least had only recently read it *closely*. He had a lot to say about the biography as a biography, but I remember that he was particularly disturbed by the dismissive treatment of Rothko by some of the "young Turks" of the pop art world (Rothko in turn loathed their work):

> . . . *I knew some of those artists . . . a little . . . not well . . . but they behaved badly to their . . . ELDERS . . . we all had wildly inconsistent natures. . . . Many of us . . . the usual arrogance . . . the usual . . . egos . . . the usual . . . EVERYTHING . . . But you have to have figures LARGER THAN YOURSELF . . . I guess in that regard . . . you could say that Milton Resnick was my Rothko—my Rothko-figure . . . an old-world figure . . . almost an OLD TESTAMENT figure . . . "in the spaces between heartbeat, you hear ancestral voices. . . ." That kind of figure. . . . Anyway, the Rothko biography . . . !!!!!!!!!!!! . . . had me up half the night. . . . The dark side of the art world stuff . . . but more importantly the dark side of the soul . . . the horrendous inner mental turmoil . . . that Rothko experienced ("his mind a shtetl with only ghosts left in it" Milton said) in exhibiting work. . . . The late "dark" paintings . . . to me . . . are not about DEPRESSION . . . at all. . . . They are about THE IMPOSSIBILITY OF BEING . . . but you have to still BE -- ALL THAT OLD WORLD SADNESS . . . illness that awaited him and . . . finally . . . the EXHAUSTION. . . . There's that one part in the book . . . where Rothko sits with Elaine de Kooning . . . all night while she rewrites an article about their . . . contemporaries . . . he sort of hovers near by . . . sentinel . . . he goes out for pastrami sandwiches. . . . He looks at the essay not quite but almost . . . sentence by sentence . . . all that insecurity but wanting her to write ACCURATELY . . . but you know, I think . . . Rothko was wrong asking her to erase some stuff about Milton Avery's . . . "influence" on him . . . even a sentence! That seems confused . . . to me it seems*

confused . . . I mean DEFINITELY the influence is there . . .
maybe he simply didn't want Elaine de Kooning to say it in
print . . . all so strange . . . complicated . . . don't you think . . .

In one of many letters Jake composed while receiving chemo-therapy treatments, he wrote: *. . . writing a letter distracts me . . .*
gets me out of self-pity . . . a letter's like a visit . . . said Katherine
Mansfield in that book you sent . . . remember? . . .

The last postcard I got from Jake arrived on December 26, 2014, four days before he died; it consisted of just a quote from Simone Weil: *Friendship is the desired, necessary, and often urgent discourse between two solitudes.*

But the final letter I received in fact arrived on Monday, December 29; it was in a package along with the framed photograph of Émile Bernard and Vincent van Gogh.

Dear Howard . . . post script to our telephone conversation . . .
a good CONVERSATION . . . sorry I was so tired . . . breath-
ing poorly . . . here. . . . Thinking of dear Milton . . . thinking
of Guston . . . "representation can't always be of recognizable
Things . . ."

Beautiful poems . . . Jane's . . . I read some Rilke and
Adorno . . . Here's my SELF-PORTRAIT—three sweaters . . .
Woodburning . . . Stove . . . Still not warm enough . . . human
but not . . . A BEING . . . But good clear THINKING . . .
looking forward to your visit . . . I know you as . . . I continue
to know you . . . as one of my blessings . . . alone one hour not
the . . . next . . . (with cat) . . . let's talk soon. I SHOULD
HAVE moved next door in Vermont . . . you should have
moved next door . . . here!!!!!!!!!

Love, Jake

ASHTON'S OAK
(DIARY OF
A PAINTING)

Thereabouts 4 a.m., no hint of morning light yet, I would have to say that we were both wired on no-sleep and caffeine. "Hey, remember this?" Jake said, handing me a piece of graph paper. And I did remember the page, which was part of a loose-knit folder having to do with a large painting called *Ashton's Oak*.

The underlying grid for *Ashton's Oak* was set down in October of 2009; I had seen the canvas leaning against a wall in Jake's studio, surrounded by three pencil and charcoal studies. A fourth was added in late winter, on which Jake had written in pencil, *Dusk occurred as if in a daydream, when sunlight perhaps held inside a tree for a century finally revealed itself.* The quote was from William Bartram, botanist-artist, who was best known for his chronicle of travels in the southern British colonies in North America from 1777 to 1779.

Here is my diary of watching Jake paint *Ashton's Oak.*

JUNE 30, 2010

Last evening at dinner, Jake offered up the idea about my observing *Ashton's Oak* as he completed it. "But the deal would be, you'd have to read me a book," he said. "You know, in between and around talking about everything else." He got up and found a book on the shelf and handed it to me. *The Autobiography of Vincent van Gogh* (480 pages, including letters to his brother). "I've owned that book maybe ten years, but for some reason, I only dipped into it now and then," Jake said. Tucked into the pages was a bookmark from Strand Bookstore.

This morning after breakfast, I looked at a few studies for *Ashton's Oak* at the kitchen table. When I went out to the studio, Jake was already at work. There was lots of birdsong just outside the studio. I carried in a cup of coffee, set the tape cassette on a table between me and Jake, sat quite a ways back from the tripod. Right away he said, "Let's not talk for a while," which I liked because it meant silence and brushstrokes were being recorded and I could just watch. He was working on the thick, wide limb at the upper left of the canvas. On the desk alongside brushes in jars was a large wooden breadboard; on its roughhewn surface were individual globs and admixtures of gold, butterscotch, sepia, black, flaxen, honey, dandelion, and mustard paint, which were to me transmutable elements as mysterious as an alchemist's, an analogy I probably allowed myself because the figure of the oak in *Ashton's Oak*—at this point in the painting, Jake said, "the dimensions of the tree are set, there's a lot of work left"—suggested a large nude figure made of gold and almost camouflaged in a forest by a kind of liquid flooding sunlight.

After a little more than an hour, Jake set down his brush and carried the canvas to the paint-splotched empty wall of the studio and hung it on a nail. He then sat in a red canvas chair and just looked at the painting for a good hour more. I wasn't invited to this and one should never go where one is not invited. In fact, when Jake took the painting to the wall, I'd gone to the storage drawer and took out some of the studies, got a new cassette from my overnight bag, went to the house to get a refill of coffee and listen to CBC radio. I wanted to catch up on Canadian news.

When I returned to the studio, I saw that Jake had placed a second canvas chair in front of *Ashton's Oak*. He waved me over. I brought the recorder with me and set it on the floor, also paint-splotched. We both looked at the painting for a while, until he said, "The painting needs a lot of work. I finally see I've been channeling van Gogh, though this isn't his yellow. But something to do with the . . . visceral . . . provocation of a particular color."

"Not sure I understand," I said. "I mean, a lot of your trees have a kind of inner light, even the darker ones."

"Yeah, but with *this* painting, it goes back to Bartram, see? 'A full vessel of light.' I don't want this oak to seem . . . ignited. I want to evoke saved-up light, light from a lot of years . . . maybe even a century. Reminds me of the Jackson Mac Low poems you sent me."

"*22 Light Poems*," I said.

"I love those poems. The most common of objects giving off their own light. I like the way he dedicated different kinds of light to different friends."

Silence for a good fifteen minutes, then Jake carried the canvas back to its tripod, sat on an elevated bench, and started to work again. I figured this was a good time to take up *Dear Theo* and start reading aloud. To which Jake said, "Okay, good." The first letter was dated *London, June 1873*. Three pages in, I came to this passage: "I send you a little drawing. I made it last Sunday, the morning when the little daughter of my landlady died. It is a view on Streatham Common, a large grassy plain with oak trees and gorse. As you see, it is stretched on the title-page of 'Poems' by Edmond Roche. There are some very fine ones among them, grave and sad. I copy them out for you."

At which moment Jake said, "'I copy them out for you.' Wow, it's like Vincent's the last surviving example of almost a pre-Gutenberg patience, right there. Vincent is so devoted to his brother. You get that in just a few pages. It's really heartbreaking."

As Jake worked on the painting, I continued through the first forty pages of *Dear Theo*, the Plume Edition published in paperback in 1995. In his introduction dated January 6, 1937, the editor of the first US edition, Irving Stone (author of *Lust for Life*, a biography of van Gogh; Kirk Douglas portrayed van Gogh in the 1956 biopic, and Anthony Quinn portrayed Gauguin) wrote, "After Johanna van Gogh's death in 1927, Vincent's manuscripts became property of V. W. van Gogh, Johanna and Theo's son. V. W. van Gogh has given the blessing of the van Gogh family to this project, on which I have been working since 1937, at which time I began studying Vincent's letters for material for 'Lust for Life.' It has been my purpose to keep in every line Vincent wrote that has retained its beauty, significance, and importance, and to eliminate the countless pages of repetition, unimportant detail and comment which have since lost both meaning and value. My aim has been to edit the 1670 pages of material down to a swiftly flowing, continuous, normal-sized book . . ."

When I had read this by lamplight in the guest room the previous night, my first response, apart from gratefulness for Stone's gargantuan labor of editing, and my hesitant nod to the concerns of a New York publisher about accessibility, was that certain things struck me as dubious. ". . . a swiftly flowing, continuous, normal-sized book" resulted in the hundreds of Vincent's *individual* letters (1873–1890) to be shaped and presented in narrative aggregates—Book I, Book II, Book III, Book IV—and the entire epic volume was given a subtitled, therefore a literary, intent not chosen by Vincent: "autobiography." My fit of pique too was about ". . . to eliminate the countless pages of repetition, unimportant details and comment . . ." I thought, hey, wait a minute, Vincent wasn't writing a novel in which repetition indeed might have impeded narrative flow; who was Irving Stone, anyway, to determine that repetition wasn't a key ingredient to a complete and honest portrait of Vincent van Gogh's days and nights? In fact, I eventually found that in certain of even the edited letters, repetition is the metronome of Vincent's obsessiveness and anxiety. I felt that the full extent of all of Vincent's epistolary moods should be considered sacrosanct. I cannot really say why I got so agitated about all of this—it may have been due to a second and third whiskey—but I did. Yet during coffee before Jake went to the studio, when I voiced my disgruntlement, Jake said, "It's okay, my friend, it's okay. I mean, I can't know what the originals were anyway, so I'm not going to get worked up about it." However, I did agree with Stone that Vincent was "endowed with one of the most comprehensive gifts of understanding and expression it has ever been the burden of one man to carry." Of course, it could be said that Stone's fictional portrait of van Gogh read like a portrait of the biblical Job.

I went on to another letter, which van Gogh wrote in The Hague, December 1881: "Dear brother, you comprise, in my isolation, so often the art of memory itself. I have been thinking of you very often lately, and also of that time long ago when you visited The Hague, and we walked together along the Ryswyk Road and drank milk at that mill. It may be that this has influenced me somehow when making these drawings, in which I have tried to draw things as naively as possible, exactly as I saw them before me."

"Well, he succeeded in that, didn't he?" Jake said. "I'd like to succeed in that."

After 64 pages, I had to stop reading. I set the book down.

"Oh, man, it's nearly three o'clock," Jake said. "Plus it's goddamned exhausting being with Vincent. One intense dude, right? Let's go in and make some sandwiches. But now that I've got Vincent on the brain, let me ask you something. You know that photograph of van Gogh sitting outdoors with his great friend Émile Bernard?"

"How could I not know that photograph, Jake? You've spoken about it maybe ten thousand times. Also, it's hanging on the guest room wall, remember?"

"...never can put enough thought into that photograph," Jake said. "But let me ask you something ... what do you think because what I think is, that photograph'd be less ... haunting ... if we could actually see Vincent's face."

"Maybe it's like Freud's idea that the power is in the withholding," I said. "I mean the power of the photograph itself. I hardly think the photographer—whoever it was—I hardly think the photographer was withholding anything on purpose. He just snapped the picture. It was the photograph the situation allowed—the perspective that was allowed. You told me nothing's really known about who took it, right? But the fact of it being sourced as a photograph of Bernard and van Gogh, that has to indicate that the photographer probably knew whom he was taking a picture of, but who can ever know for sure? I think you and me should fly to Amsterdam and do some research and find out some stuff. How about next month?"

"Knowing you, you aren't kidding. But I might still be working on this painting next month."

"I hadn't thought of that."

"Sometimes I look at the photograph and try to get behind Émile Bernard's eyes and imagine what Vincent looked like that day. I try to imagine the state of Vincent's health ... even the state of his mind. It's like a weird daydream or something. Let's go make some lunch."

Lunch, then Jake took a nap, and I drove around, just to take in village life in Accord and over in neighboring Stone Ridge. I am never bored; Samuel Pepys said boredom is stupidity, and I agree. There were always things to look at. Trees.

I made a basic basil and tomato sauce for linguini, and sauteed a choice of toppings, mushrooms, finely chopped sausage, finely cut pieces of scallion, and of course there was a small bowl of parmesan cheese, freshly grated. During the meal, we watched the DVD of *Voyager*, the film based on Max Frisch's novel, *Homo*

Faber. After the film, we each had a whiskey. Jake settled in to make some phone calls, whereas I went out to the studio. I looked at *Ashton's Oak* awhile, then crashed by 10 p.m.

JULY 1

I was woken by a noise at 4 a.m. I threw on some clothes and walked through the storage room to the corridor, and down the corridor I saw a goose-necked lamp was on, and so was a floor lamp. Jake, wearing jeans and a tee shirt, and barefooted, was sitting in his canvas chair, looking at *Ashton's Oak* on the wall. I caught another couple hours of sleep, then went into the house and made mush-room omelets. I carried a tray with the omelets and a pot of coffee out to the studio, where Jake and I had a mostly silent breakfast, as we both looked at the painting. Yet, needless to say, his looking was not my looking. I almost uttered the most inane words possible, *The painting looks finished*; instead I said, "It's really changed so much since yesterday," which sounded equally inane.

"It's all hubris, memory, and quarrelsome desire until it's com-pleted," he said. "That's Kitaj talking."

Jake went in for a shower and to make a phone call or two. I stayed in the studio. I think it was about 9:30 a.m. when Jake returned. He immediately carried *Ashton's Oak* back to the well-worn adjustable mahogany tripod. Then, without comment, he demonstrated his mood: he turned up the classical music sta-tion on the radio to hear François Couperin's "Pièces de Violes." As intensely aching, and sometimes verging on treacly, Couperin played (we shared a love of this composer)—on the tape the music almost drowns out his voice—Jake said, "With Couperin I can almost see—I won't say who, but I can almost see a woman I knew, lifting a sweater off her body—it was at a beach. It had gotten too warm for sweaters. Of course, when her head disappeared under the sweater—just for a moment—she was a torso. That's the image I can see so clearly. And that's one reason this painting

I'm working on now . . . feels a little different."

He rustled through a stack of papers and said, "Take a gander at this—"

It was an 8-by-11-inch sheet of graph paper with a drawing of a nude. "It's Japanese but I don't know who drew it," he said. I studied it a moment. "It's the same movement—that lifting movement—I'm trying to get in this oak tree. The posture of the tree. One fluid movement. One fluid upward opening movement. It's like that woman on the beach, she's my model, but not in the studio, just in thinking of her so often. That's why it's a different experience with this painting. Completely familiar—yet completely different. I don't see any contradiction, not really."

"I wish I could have the same memory, listening to Couperin," I said.

"Well, you had to be there," Jake said, laughing a little.

As the rest of the Couperin suites played, Jake shaded the tree limb that rose to the upper right of the canvas; at this juncture it was a somewhat rounded-off, truncated part of the tree, as opposed to a slightly lower limb that extended on out of the canvas. After the Couperin ended, the mood shifted; Jake turned the radio volume to low. He ran a thumb along the surface of *Ashton's Oak*, then stood back from it a few yards. "I think what's finally happening here, is the painting now seems to be originating as much from Bartram's descriptions of sunset as anything. It's never just one thing—but it's definitely Bartram. That sense of a daydream—even his word 'urgent.' Urgent yellow—urgent sepia—etcetera. Urgent conversation . . . between . . . tree light and sunset light, maybe. Yeah, I'm thinking just now . . . in a way, it feels like I'm painting William Bartram's daydream."

"Last night, I was looking at some of the studies for this painting," I said.

"Yeah, but even if I'd done a hundred studies, really, I never know where it's going to go until it goes there. It *evolves*, right? With this painting, the colors are sort of continuous from tree to background, from background to tree, and the outline of the tree itself has to be done just right, so that the tree might seem to be—*materializing* . . . coming into view . . . something like that. It's not quite there yet . . ."

Work continued for many an hour on the upper right, and then the entire left side of the painting. I realized that, on the radio, it was a whole program dedicated to Couperin. But the music was now so faint it seemed it could scarcely make it to this century.

"You know that photograph," Jake said.

"I can't possibly imagine which photograph you mean," I said.

"Very funny. Would you mind getting it from the guest room?"

"Not at all."

I carried in the framed photograph (a facsimile) of Émile Bernard and Vincent van Gogh and propped it up on the desk nearest the tripod. Jake took *Ashton's Oak* to the far wall again. He then sat in front of the photograph. "At first, I didn't take much notice of the trees in the background and to the left," he said. "The trees in two places behind the stone wall. Or this one farthest on the left that you can hardly make out. But, actually, there's quite a few scraggly trees, aren't there. The two men have heavy coats on, so I think it might be winter."

"Do you know anything about their friendship?" I said. "I don't."

"Bernard and van Gogh's? I read some things, in some book or other. I read a little about Asnières, where the photograph was taken. Bernard's family had a house there and van Gogh visited there. What I do remember is that after Vincent moved to the south of France, they kept up their friendship. Vincent wrote him some amazing letters about painting. And when you look at Bernard's own paintings, you see van Gogh and Cézanne everywhere in them—he wasn't very *original*. I think of something

Resnick said of another painter—'His originality is elusive.'
Bernard was friends with van Gogh and Cézanne—closest with
Gauguin. He championed them both. Bernard wrote a few plays
and lots of critical stuff about art—he had a reputation."

"You know something? When I was making the artist-model
drawings over about twenty years' time, I did some sketches that
respond to this photograph of Bernard and van Gogh, but I never
really completed a drawing, but in the sketches there were two

figures, and one was always hunched over and shrouded. I think in one drawing the hunched-over guy was an angel, maybe in a black overcoat, like Bruno Ganz in *Wings of Desire*. But always there were two men at a café table. Sometimes there'd be a tree, too."

Jake worked for a few moments and said, "I think Vincent was living in The Hague, right?" I got the hint and started to read from *Dear Theo* and read a number of pages up to where van Gogh writes,

> *I made a large drawing with the crayon you sent me, combined with lithographic chalk. It is a digger—my model was the little odd almshouse man. His bald head, bent over the black earth, seemed to me full of a certain significance, for instance, "In the sweat of thy face shalt thou eat bread." The drawings of the woman with the spade and this digger have such an aspect that one will not think they are made in some way, but rather will not think at all about how they are made. By certain grey tints, by a certain richness and pith in the black, one avoids that dull and metallic aspect of the ordinary Conte pencil. And these little things are in my opinion worth the trouble of seeking for such materials as crayon and lithographic chalk.*

"He was so grateful just to get a pencil from his brother," Jake said. "And here I can just call up the art supply store and paints and brushes and everything will be delivered right to my door. Speaking of that, I have to go to New Paltz, to run some errands. Want to come with?"

We got into Jake's car and as he steered down the street, he said, "But you know, once you noticed those trees along the left side of the photograph—you know, the ones behind the stone wall—you can't ever not notice them."

I thought, if these last two days of conversation were a letter, I wouldn't edit out a single word about the Bernard–van Gogh photograph, not a single repetition. We had a great laughing afternoon in New Paltz; Jake purchased graph paper and two wooden rulers, sent boxes by UPS; we took in a movie, *The King's Speech*. We got some Italian takeout and once back on the road to Accord, Jake said, "The thing is, the photographer had to have told *somebody* it was Vincent van Gogh and Émile, because, I mean, how else would we have them identified in the public record today— in books about van Gogh, for instance? But I've always wondered if Vincent himself ever saw the photograph." Silence a moment; search for the classical music station on the car radio. "Probably not, though. When you really think about it, Vincent probably never saw it."

JULY 2

After breakfast, Jake decided to work on a tree drawing. He carried a chair to the woods behind his house and set up there. I decided to look yet again at the studies that led up to *Ashton's Oak*, this time in chronological order, and record this or that thought without Jake having to suffer my unlettered observations. It all just felt like a once-in-a-lifetime thing to do. In the studio, I set out all the studies on a table. One thing I had learned over the past decade was that a "study" didn't necessarily mean a drawing composed *before* its namesake painting, though in the case of *Ashton's Oak*, Jake did no drawings of it once the painting was completed. Jake had great interest in a book by Susan Grace Galassi, a curator at the Frick, which discussed how Picasso kept with certain subjects in his drawings well after said subject was painted—Picasso had said, "The line of thought, nor the obsession, doesn't always end with the painting." The momentum of the imagination keeps going, and along the way, a painting is part of that. This isn't necessarily a surprising or revelatory practice but is nonetheless compelling to think about. For example, I have two of Jake's drawings titled *Study for Spring Birch*—now, the actual painting *Spring Birch* was completed in 2005, but one of the two studies is dated 2006 and the other 2007. Indeed, compositionally they are slight variations on the painting itself, but rather than seeing this as a kind of esoteric footnote, I think it is exactly what Picasso described, a kind of ongoingness of thought.

At about 11:30 a.m. Jake came into the studio and said, "There's a library book sale over in Stone Ridge. Tables of books set out in front. It's just a ten-minute drive on 209."

"Jake, no kidding, I was in that library yesterday, when I was driving around," I said. "It's such an elegant old building. The way libraries should look."

"Let's go."

Then, that photograph again. In the car, I had the cassette recorder, and the second I switched it on, Jake said, "The thing about that photograph is, I mean—and this is so obvious—you work on a painting and no matter if you'd had a kind of *idée fixe* for months, the painting can change at any given moment. But look at that photograph—snap—two seconds. Maybe the photographer studied it like a . . . *tableau vivant* . . . for years . . . or maybe not. But look at its composition. Can you imagine standing in the darkroom and that composition comes into focus?"

We could see the Stone Ridge Library up ahead; people were milling about the tables and, delightfully, there was a string quartet of young musicians, dressed in formal black and white.

"Ever think of arranging for a sarcophagus, Jake—when the time comes?" I said. "You know, maybe fifty years from now when you die. Have some local carpenter build it, you could paint hieroglyphs on it yourself—you could write yourself a letter for Eternity on the inside walls. You could demand that the Bernard–van Gogh photograph be put in there—along your journey to the next life."

"As long as I could wrap it in my ratty old brown sweater," he said, "the one I've had since about 1970."

"I'm fairly certain the contents would be up to you," I said.

It was a warm and sunny day in Stone Ridge. The quartet was performing Haydn. I started to browse various field guides to birds, moths, flowers, and fish, and then moved on to the somewhat meager selection of books on photography, as I was always on the lookout for books for Emma who, at age 22, was already devoted to the art. Jake went to the next table over, full of art books. I saw him pick up a large orange-covered book, open it, and read maybe a page or two. He looked over at me with an odd expression on his face that I couldn't read. After another half hour or so of browsing, Jake brought five books to the checkout table, whereas I ended up empty-handed. In the car he said, "I think I'm going to actually finish up the painting today. It's just the sense I have of it. But who knows, it's been months already. It might take another year! When we get back, I'd like to be out in the studio alone. Come out around seven, okay?"

Late that afternoon, using Jake's Olivetti manual that was in the guest room, I typed a few letters and read *Aracoeli* by Elsa Morante and listened to some Bach partitas played by András Schiff. I took a nap. When I woke, I saw it was 7:15. I found Jake at work on the lower part of the trunk of the oak. "This section needed something," he said. He nodded at *Dear Theo*. I read, oh, maybe twenty more pages, then Jake said, "Go on into the house and fix something for dinner. I'm going to keep working."

"I've got to get up to Saratoga," I said. "I start to teach tomorrow."

"Oh, yeah, forgot," he said. "Why not drive down in a few days again?"

"That'd be fine."

I went back to the guest room, packed up, and carried my overnight bag out to the car. In the studio, good-byes. He was touching up the top right branch. Jake said, "You know what I want for Vincent? I want him to be able to walk into the van Gogh museum in Amsterdam. I want him to be able to just stand there—Vincent the ghost. I want the museum to be packed full. I want Vincent's voice to suddenly bring everything to a standstill. I want every astonished visitor to hear him say really loud, 'My brother Theo believed in me! I might have been stark raving mad but I was *alive!* Look at what's on these walls. I was *alive!*'"

In about an hour and a half, when I got to the Surrey-Williamson Inn across from the Skidmore campus, I sat on the bed in Room 5 and was about to eat a sandwich I'd purchased for dinner and then prepare for the next day's fiction workshop. I realized I'd left some papers in the car and when I went out to retrieve them, I noticed what was clearly the orange-covered book Jake had purchased in Stone Ridge: *Vincent van Gogh: Letters to Émile Bernard.* He had not mentioned this book to me! Clearly it was the book that had brought such a strange and puzzled expression to his face. Now, one thing I can say for certain, Jake loathed bombastic assertions of synchronicity in life—he would reject there being anything thought-provoking about his finding this book.

The telephone rang about 9 p.m. "Hey, it's Jake."

"At the library sale I saw you pick up the book," I said first thing.

"It wasn't any goddamn stupid Jungian coincidence mystical thing."

"That's hardly what I'd suggest, is it."

We both had a good laugh.

"I bet they're amazing letters," I said.

"Filled to the brim with all sorts of subjects, knowing Vincent," Jake said. "Full of him trying to sustain a friendship, knowing him. Full of painting. Send me the book back once you've read it, okay? Then I'll send it back when I'm done."

"Nice to hang out in the studio so much, Jake. I won't forget it."
Brief silence.

"I've finished the painting," he said. "Pretty sure, though I'll look at it in the morning. It's on the back wall again. I'll look at it in the morning."

"You'll determine then, right?"

"Yeah, when I look at it in the morning."

CHAPTER 7

WHEN WAS THE LAST TIME YOU TALKED ALL NIGHT

Finally, we got out to the studio.

Somewhere near 7:30 a.m. I had put on a pot of coffee. "The strange thing," Jake said, "is that sometimes I sit here and think, Jake, you're dying, and in a way—hypothetically, at least—you can try and choose the last thing you want to look at."

"Would it be those trees just off the porch?"

Jake gave an exaggerated shrug of his shoulders and got very quiet. I felt pretty stupid in the moment, that my suggestion could only be crude guesswork. It's just that we had been sitting in silence looking out at trees off the porch, just enough moon and snow light to see them by. The sound of shifting logs in the wood stove annoyed the cat, who went to sit on Jake's bed. Leaning back on the sofa, Jake continued, "I mean, obviously I probably won't have a choice. But I'd prefer to just pick up a book and look at a picture and then say, 'I love this Cézanne, okay, now Lord, God, Krishna, Navajo priest chanting the Blessingway, Buddha, I'm not picky—whoever might be paying attention, Okay, it's time, let me go! Let me go!'"

"Why not give that a shot?" I said. "You have a lot of books on Cézanne."

"I might. I just might."

"You wouldn't have to be alone in it."

"Maybe being alone is the whole idea. Besides, Howard, you stay here, it'd be like having a turkey vulture sitting up on that shelf, near where Milton's painting is. Waiting. Okay, sure, a vulture who'd drink coffee nonstop. A vulture who's a dear friend. You get what I mean, right?"

"What's this vulture to think?" I said. "Sees a man stumbling around in five sweaters and a knit hat, clutching a book of Cézanne paintings. The vulture might think, 'I'm definitely in the right place . . .'"

Jake fell into a seismic laughter, which unfortunately led to a kind of gasping, and it seemed he couldn't catch his breath. I was ready to call 911. But then he said, "God, Buddha, Navajo priest—it's time . . ." Gulping water from a glass I'd handed him, Jake said, "Hey, do you remember those two women at the Met that time?" His breathing noticeably steadied. "The two elderly women—the painting they were looking at is in that fat book on Cézanne right over there. Bring it over, will you? Are you cold? I'm cold. Can you put another log on?"

I handed Jake the Cézanne book and then put two logs on the fire. "They were looking at this"—he held up the book to the open page—"*Still-Life With Apples and a Pot of Primroses*," he said.

Speaking of *Still-Life with Apples and a Pot of Primroses*. If I remember correctly, it was in July 2003, I'd had a weekend break during a residency at the New York State Writers Institute, the only time I taught two weeks instead of one, and had taken the train from Saratoga Springs to New York to meet Jake. He had galleries to visit, a doctor's appointment, and I think a visit with Naoto Nakagawa. Finally, we met up at the Metropolitan Museum where we had coffee together and then wandered off in different directions, but with the understanding that we'd meet in an hour and a half at the front entrance. But after about an hour, I noticed a small gathering of people in front of *Still-Life with Apples and a Pot of Primroses*. A docent had just concluded her spiel. Two elderly women—and by this I mean in their mid-eighties, at best guess—didn't move on with the docent's group. One of the women was dressed in an expensive-looking cashmere coat, a beautiful black begonia-print dress, a pearl necklace, black velvet fingerless gloves, and her white hair was tucked up under a beret. By comparison, her companion struck me as poor relations—I'm not making judgement, just describing: she had on a coat that appeared right off the rack, a frumpy sack-dress of some sort, and appeared distinctly unkempt; her own white hair only half organized and held by a plastic barrette consisting of a line of cat faces. As I stood behind them, Jake stepped up next to me, and just as he did, the woman in the cashmere coat said, "My goodness, how could he have captured those apples so perfectly? What genius." Taking a moment to consider both the painting and her friend's comment, the woman in the less remarkable coat said, "What I'm looking at is the painting of someone who knew what it was like to be hungry." The cashmere-coated woman replied, "Oh, of course, my dear, you'd have to take every opportunity to lord your personal experiences over me, wouldn't you?" The friends sauntered off arm in arm.

"I choose *Bend in the Forest Road*," Jake said. "I understand that I won't be standing in front of the original, but I can maybe be staring at my poster of it." I knew that the poster hung in the guest room.

"So you just made your choice then," I said.

"Yeah, *Bend in the Forest Road*."

When we returned to Jake's home, I went right out to the studio and brought back in the framed poster. "Lean it up against my bedroom wall, will you?" he said. "I can look at it from bed."

Whenever I was out in Jake's studio, I always found myself reading the walls, which contained a veritable anthology of aphorisms, quotes, and poems, some written out on a piece of paper and thumbtacked or taped to the wall, but many written directly on the wall itself. ". . . Sometimes I touch them like a mezuzah," he once said, as if they had some ancient protective quality. Jake's studio walls were literary; you could read them. *Life is not long enough for art, nor long enough for friendship*—Emerson. That was written on a wall near a bookshelf in the storage room. Near the radio on the shelf in the guest room, *We may climb into the thin and cold realm of pure geometry and lifeless science or sink into that of sensation. Between these extremes, is the equator of life, of thought, of spirit, of poetry—a narrow belt*, also from Emerson. (Jake sometimes signed his letters, *with love, here at the equator.*) On the wall near the entrance to the studio was written a quote from Chuang Tzu: *In the state of pure experience, we have no intellectual knowledge of any kind.* And written on yet another wall, a complete Navajo blessing or prayer:

In beauty, may we walk
All day long, may we walk
with the returning seasons, may we walk—
Beautifully may we possess again,
Beautifully birds, beautifully joyous birds

On the path marked with pollen, may we walk
With grasshoppers about our feet, may we walk—
In beauty may we walk—
With beauty before us, may we walk—
With beauty behind us, may we walk—
With beauty above us, may we walk—
With beauty all arounds us, may we walk

In old age, wandering on the trail of beauty,
Living again, may we walk—

In old age, wandering on the trail of beauty,
Lively, may we walk—
It is finished in beauty
It is finished in beauty

Jake picked up a copy of a 1961 collection of Resnick's poetry, *Up and Down*, from the table in front of the sofa. He read aloud the poem titled "I fell," a severely ironic choice, considering Jake's own terribly injurious fall from a tree:

I fell from a fork
in a branch
of wonder
tree who parted laboring leaves
straight to eternity
days depart
I sing
Laughing sound of land
in green
open office
from play I who fell
branchofatree
a fork to wonder to part
sing

"God almighty, Milton was a terrible poet," Jake said. "But in 1961, poets were painters, painters were poets, everybody tried everything. Milton was a good reader of poetry, he was always talking about this or that poet. There's what?—two or three collections of Milton's poems out there. He was a serious writer, though. He took it seriously. He was always writing something. But a lot of the poems—I mean, talk about convoluted! I read them all the time and to this day I don't get a lot past the imagery. But the images can be very provocative. No denying that. I mean, he was a Jewish painter, his whole history was the sacredness of the word—he painted in an old synagogue, for God's sake!" Jake was laughing and coughing, and for the moment laughter won out.

I adjusted the cassette recorder. "All these years," I said, "I never knew how you first met Milton Resnick."

"Can you put on some tea? Dry throat," he said. "I know I've talked about Milton a lot with you over the years. Plus I took you to 87 Eldridge to meet him once. You met Pat Passlof, Milton's wife, that time, too." I served us tea. After a few sips, Jake said, "I mean, from the start, Milton was important to me. Up until the day he died that was true. It still is true. People have conjectured all sorts of things about our friendship and everything I ever heard thirdhand was wrong. After he killed himself, I went to say a final good-bye and I couldn't. There were too many people and maybe—I'd have to think more about this—too much emotion. But we never had a falling out. It's true there were long periods of time we didn't see each other, but that sort of thing happens in a long friendship, right? One year I'd see Milton a lot and then two years'd go by. But I carried Milton everywhere with me. What's that Yannis Ritsos line?—something like 'separate precinct of the heart.' That's where Milton lives.

"Basically, it was through a painter named Bob Hoagie that I first got to know Milton, though I may have met him separately from Bob, I don't remember. In New York, in my twenties, I was studying with Bob Hoagie. There's some photographs somewhere. Bob was a good painter, I thought. He was a very knowledgeable painter and I felt lucky to be studying with him. But one thing was clear was how influenced his own painting was by Milton's painting. I guess you could say blatantly influenced. Bob knew a lot about painting and had an interesting mind, and worked hard at his own painting, Well, sometimes, with some painters—they never can completely work through their primary influences. I'm not suggesting this was finally the case with Bob Hoagie. I'm just saying that I never personally saw him work through and past Milton's influence. And Bob just sort of disappeared. He faded away, at least from the art scene I was aware of. I lost track of him.

"At the time, Milton's sister had a gallery on 13th Street. The Feiner Gallery. 13th and 5th Avenue and I had a few shows there. Maybe I was too young to have those shows. But I was ambitious and excited about it all. There was some notice taken. I can't remember what the reviews were if there were any and all of that, but I felt generally encouraged, I guess. And I was very much influenced by Milton's work. By his whole ethos. By his intensity and his thinking. I held his work in high esteem. Like him I was appalled when Pop Art hit the scene. I found much of it loathsome. Some of it had great energy but I couldn't locate any compelling life force in it. Milton just plain hated it. Really, I didn't want anything to do with Pop Art. I wasn't as much baffled as disinterested. Milton fumed against it. And when he fumed, he really fumed.

"Somewhere in that period Milton moved to New Mexico, for a lot of personal reasons. And in some ways, I kept emulating his paintings. But the thing about such an original painter as Milton, is you can really only emulate. It was kind of tormenting. Not kind of—it was tormenting."

At this point I could see that Jake looked a touch distracted, perhaps by his own fatigue. "Let's get back to this later," I said.

"Yeah, but—well, I've been thinking back, thinking back, thinking back," he said. "It wears me out sometimes. Strange how that works. It's like there's too much history. But see those notebooks on the counter? I want you to have those. Take them home with you. Bring one over, will you?"

I set two hardback notebooks on the table and Jake opened the one with the black cover. I saw on the first lineless page, DREAMING THAT I WENT WITH LU AND YU TO VISIT YUAN CHEN.

I read this out loud and said, "What's this from?"

"It's by Po Chü-i, ancient Chinese guy who wrote some good stuff on the subject of friendship," Jake said. "Arthur Waley translated him. Annie Dillard at Yale put me on to his poetry. To ancient Chinese poetry in general. Turn a few pages, there's a poem with the word 'Dreaming' in the title, I think."

I found "Dreaming That I Went With Lu and Yu to Visit Yuan Chen" and read it aloud.

> At night I dreamt I was back in Ch'ang-an;
> I saw again the faces of old friends.
> And in my dreams, under an April sky,
> They led me by the hand to wander in the spring winds.
> Together we came to the village of Peace and Quiet.
> We stopped our horses at the gate of Yuan Chen.
> Yuan Chen was sitting all alone.
> When he saw me coming, a smile came to his face.
> He pointed back at the flowers in the western court,
> Then opened wine in the northern summer-house.
> He seemed to be saying that neither of us had changed;
> He seemed to be regretting that joy will not stay;
> That our souls had met only for a little while,
> To part again with hardly time for greeting.
> I woke up and thought him still at my side;
> I put out my hand; there was nothing there at all.

"That poem always gets to me," Jake said. "I wrote it out on the studio wall. It's behind a stack of books now, I think."

Paging through the black notebook, I saw the drawings sponsored by the Po Chü-i dreamscape elegy were calligraphic in nature, but there were also human figures embraced in farewells, or perhaps greetings. One drawing depicted Yuan Chen sitting alone.

I took up the second notebook, this one with a magenta cover. On the title page, stanzas from a poem by Paul Blackburn (1926–1971), which I read aloud:

How we move
about the wealth
of friendships;
too often at the edges of it

How rare we move to center,
where we live.

"I met Blackburn a couple times—1960s," Jake said. "There were a lot of readings at St. Marks-in-the-Bowery. Blackburn hung out at McSorley's pub, I remember. Traditional ale house on 7th Avenue. I was there a few times. Blackburn was a real New York poet, but he'd been to Spain—and I think to Cuba at one point. He translated Lorca and Julio Cortázar's novels and stories. Very hip sort of guy, and those stanzas always got to me, too. I wrote them on the wall somewhere—where—maybe the guest room—maybe now behind a bookshelf, not sure." Jake sipped some tea. "You and me—right now—we might've moved . . . *to center.*"

When I replied, "Let's stay there as long as possible," I had no concern how sentimental or otherwise over-the-top it may have sounded; that Horace quote comes to mind: *Why should I be ashamed or exercise control / Mourning so dear a soul.* Anyway, it seemed that the Blackburn stanzas had wise and instructive qualities, and I was glad I'd then said, "You could reconsider my staying on here for a while."

Jake stretched out his arms, tucked his head low into his sweaters, and released a brief, guttural screech; this apparently was his imitation of a vulture. "Very funny," I said. I could still see stars through the trees. I don't think we said another word for a good half hour or even longer.

Jake dozed off and I paged through the Blackburn notebook drawings. On each page, the word CENTER is present, and there are many hovering angels. Jake, with a deep, ratcheting inhale and exhale, woke, and said, "Let's try and get out to the studio."

So we tried that again. There could be no hesitation; we had to act on the concept itself, as Jake's physical capacity could fail at any moment. "Okay," I said, "but it's cold as Hell out. We have to get you bundled up."

"I'm not a goddamned invalid," he said. "I've got sweaters on, this coat."

"Put on the fleece vest, okay?"

He took off his coat, zipped on the vest, then put the coat on again. "The studio heat should be on," he said.

I brought in two scarves and Jake wrapped them around his neck. He put on gloves, stepped out of his slippers and with effort fit into ankle-high fleece-collared boots. The effort made him sit on the sofa again. When he stood up he said, "Dizzy." We stood there propped against each other.

I'd say it took ten minutes to get to the door. "It feels like all these clothes weigh more than I do," he said. Opening the door, there was a rush of cold air. We moved ever-so-slowly toward the studio. I remember thinking, this feels reckless, and necessary. It occurred to me that I'd forgotten to put on my overcoat. It sounded as if Jake couldn't catch his breath; what he managed to say, each word carried on a wheeze, seemed a startling non sequitur: "I'm sorry you didn't get to see me happy with Kristin. I'm sorry you never saw me happy in that way. We all should've taken that ferry to Nova Scotia like we talked about. The ferry out of Bar Harbor. Like we talked about."

"We were in touch, Jake," I said. "There were letters. I knew how you were feeling."

Once inside the building, there was the hallway to the studio to navigate; on either side were bins and shelves of tools, all sorts of art materials, ladders. Up ahead I could see the two red Houzz director's chairs. Jake told me he once heard some art critic or other say to Milton Resnick, "Artists' studios are sacred places," a statement that in response Resnick dismissively refined, "Only if they're good painters." Jake liked to relate that anecdote.

Jake sat on a green plastic chair in front of a drafting table. He was wheezing and looked flushed. There was a T-square, a stack of music CDs, masking tape, a jar of lead pencils, a jar of charcoal pencils, a jar of pens. There were two books of Cézanne's works. Directly next to the table was an easel on which a piece of drawing paper was fastened by strips of masking tape to a board. "Finally, a human being," he said. Yet the criterion for this statement proved only to have been the sheer fact of his having physically arrived to the studio—he wasn't about to work on a drawing. That just was not going to happen. I stood back. The drawing thus far was mainly a grid, though to the right was the smudged gesture of a tree. "This was going to be a tree I saw near Lyonsville Pond," he said. The "was" struck me as wrenchingly emphatic, but I wasn't about to protest it, not then, not there. "I haven't been able to get that tree out of my head for maybe ten years."

I must report that we were in the studio all of perhaps twenty minutes. Jake stuck a few charcoal pencils into his trouser pocket. "Bring in this drawing, would you?" he said. I untaped the drawing and rolled it up and fastened it with a piece of masking tape. Then we slowly left the studio. But once outside, in order to keep us balanced, I had to leave the drawing by the door. When Jake got settled on the sofa, I went back and fetched it. I taped it so it hung off a nearby bookshelf in clear view.

Jake looked out the wide porch window and said, "Not exactly a rosy-fingered dawn, is it?" True enough; it was overcast and somewhat bleak. I heated up some coffee for myself, tea for Jake. The weasel could be seen darting in and out of the woodpile.

Again came a stretch of time without talking. This was comforting. Jake still hadn't taken off his overcoat. I put more wood in the woodstove. I sat across in the Eames chair. "That word you use all the time in your novels," he said. "That thing they say in Nova Scotia you like to use so much—*in the offing.* A storm is always in the offing. It sounds like some goddamn Victorian romance novel . . . love is in the offing, you used that word so often, it felt like in Nova Scotia there was no present tense!—something like that. Like everything's about to happen. To be honest, that phrase used to really bug me. But lately I started to appreciate it. I guess living how I'm living now, I'm grateful to have a sense of a bowl of soup in the offing."

"Yeah, I remember once in Cape Breton," I said, "standing with some people, and this woman said, 'Look there!' . . . we'd been watching a storm build up, all sorts of turbulence and mixing of clouds, blacks, grays, and seagulls going nuts. And this woman said, '. . . that storm all morning in the offing and its built up and is going to die down without even offering us any difficulties.' She almost sounded betrayed or something. Or disappointed—not to have the storm's difficulties."

"Yeah, just now, looking over at the drawing . . ." Jake finally took off his coat and laid it on the sofa—"you could say, *a tree in the offing.*"

Some silent minutes drifted by.

"When's the last time you stayed up all night talking?" I said. "I mean before last night."

"Hmmm, let me think . . . uh . . . I remember staying up talking with Guston all night," Jake said. "Maybe five of us. Somewhere in the '60s, his or my apartment, or somebody's party in New York. In those days, though, it didn't seem all that unusual to stay up all night talking. It happened all the time."

"When I taught at UCLA for a semester," I said, "late 1970s, I met Carlos Castaneda. We talked all night in a diner. I'd given a lecture—it was about Inuit soapstone carving and language and other arctic stuff, and for some reason he'd attended. He had on the most beautiful suit I'd ever seen, I think Armani, with barely visible lines. I think he was teaching or associated with the medical school in some capacity, alternative medicine. *The Teachings of Don Juan* is ethnographic fiction. But so what? It's full of good stuff nonetheless. But it was one of the most interesting conversations I'd ever had, and that's putting it mildly. Up all night in an L.A. diner and I remember him saying, 'I sometimes dream in the Aztec language.' What? For some reason, I just decided to set all my skepticism aside and thought, very cool."

"I stayed up all night talking with Milton," Jake said. "He said to come by late—what year? So I went to his studio and the next thing we knew it was morning. That was an all-night thing about painting. You walk out in the morning light, those filthy streets, and just so exhausted from somebody's mind, you know? But yeah, we talked all night. I had a lot of insomnia back then but that night wasn't insomnia."

I said, "When I was about twenty-five, I had a collapsed lung. This was in Halifax. And I somehow got into a semi-private room in the hospital. And my roommate so to speak was a woman maybe five years older than me. And neither of us could sleep, the one night she was in that room. She kept giving descriptions of children's books she was going to write. She was full of great ideas. Her character was named Tommasina Triceratops. I couldn't really hold a conversation because it was so hard for me to breathe. Now that I think about it, maybe both of us were afraid to fall asleep. Tommasina Triceratops was going to have all sorts of adventures. Me and this woman, we were both in trouble and I think we were both afraid to fall asleep. In the Respiratory Isolation Unit, I think it was called."

Exhausted, running on what seemed pure adrenaline, we were having such rare great fun, telling stories on ourselves, the world of pain seemed fallen away, of course not for long enough, but still fallen away. By now it was light outside. Then I said, "Hey, I almost forgot. I've brought you something."

I reached into my Dutch school bag. "Some old recorded versions of the 'I walk in beauty'—Navajo prayer you like so much," I said. I took out some cassettes. "A friend at the Library of Congress made copies for me."

I had brought eleven cassettes. Some were copies off wax cylinders, circa 1914, from the Hubbell Trading Post collection, recorded by Geoffrey O'Hara for the Bureau of American Ethnology at the Smithsonian Institution. Others were recorded for the Peabody Museum at Harvard University by Washington Matthews, around 1900. Still others were part of the George Herzog Collection of Navajo Blessingway cylinder recordings, from Albuquerque, New Mexico, in 1932. They had all been remastered, complete with the original scratchiness.

I put one into the cassette player I'd brought just for that purpose. For the next hour or so, we listened to variations, in the Navajo language, of the prayer written on Jake's studio wall. These timeless prayers drifting out into the surrounding trees.

Jake's comment, when the last recording ended, was, "Makes me believe in the words even more." He took some pills. I don't know what they were. "I'm going to lie down on my bed now. You going to sleep in the guest room or what?"

"I'd better get on the road, my friend."

"Okay, then," he said. "Suddenly I can hardly keep my eyes open." We embraced. "Let's talk tomorrow on the phone." He went into the bedroom. And that was it. I went out to my car where I placed the notebooks and drawings Jake had given me in the back seat. For the second time this visit I had forgotten to put on my coat. How could I be so absentminded? When I went back into the house, Jake was asleep. This time I remembered my coat.

I was heading south to Washington, DC. It was lightly snowing. When I'd driven about an hour, I pulled off at a rest stop. It just felt wrong. To my regret, I kept driving south. It felt wrong. Anyway, just to state a fact, those Navajo prayers were the last music we had listened to together. Then on December 30, the call from Verna Gillis. "But I need to tell you that Jake died this afternoon." Perhaps because literature so often provided a kind of surrogate articulation of things I could not articulate, I thought of George Eliot, *When mortal news of a friend arrives, one's heart can feel smudged in charcoal.*

AFTERWORD (BETTY)

My last visit to Jake at his home in Accord, New York? I suppose I could give you a specific date, but it was probably in September, possibly early October 2014, the year Jake died. At any rate, it was before December. I remember feeling it was good-bye. I definitely remember that.

And while I knew he was very sick, sickness was not the biggest presence, you see. No, it was that I could tell we both thought this was good-bye.

You told me, Howard, that on your own last visit, Jake was still thinking about how certain people thought that he had moved from "abstract" painting to his "realistic" painting and drawing of trees. Of course Jake always said, "The trees, I've always thought of them as abstract works. That is, they don't have photographic qualities." What did I think when I first saw his trees? I'd like to think I'm a deductive thinker; but I'm an inductive thinker. I just look at paintings and drawings and draw my conclusions from that. The looking, again and again, the looking. I guess I would say that my commitment to Jake went much deeper than seeing his work in terms of change. Having done this last show only brought home the point that the trees—that Jake was fully present in the trees, the trees felt the natural place for his painting to be. There's this wonderful quote from Jake, where he says, you know you go along and you're very popular and then all of a sudden you leave your audience and you move on and one of the things I've really treasured about Jake is his commitment to who he is as opposed to what's expected of him and that means sometimes you're letting go of the leashes that are required as a career or careerist or as a popular artist or whatever, and Jake understood this, and in talking with him, you come to really understand what a great perspective he had on himself in regard to his work. There's something that I listen to, in a video done by a group called oh God what's it called? Uh, Gorky's granddaughter—they did an interview with Jake in 2012, and at first I discounted it because it was very analytical, he was showing his grids and so on and so forth. Explaining the grids. Yet after Jake died, I realized how much he had revealed about his independence—"I don't want people dissecting my paintings for the grid and all of that; I want them to see my paintings as a whole"—and subliminally that's all I ever wanted to do too, see his paintings as a whole. I found that so interesting, because I had discounted that recorded video, and then remembered how he talked about the grids to me, you know, that he put on these glazes at different points and he saw it as a pictorial space because of the grids but finally that was all talk and wasn't painting. But he could be analytical about not being analytical about his paintings. I think also that he was completely against an analytical approach as being too easy a way to romanticize the work— or at least to intellectualize it. Still, you're right, he did philosophize, he carried on with some long metaphysical, um, meanderings, on occasion, and once in a while spoke about painting as making for a solitary life. I think he meant a solitary inner life. I say this because you asked about Jake's talking about painting as a solitary existence. All of it was interesting. He was a person of strong opinions and made unusual connections between things. It was all interesting. It was all passionate.

This idea of a solitary life, maybe being different from loneliness? Oh, yes, I recognize all of that. The first thing I ever bought was Jake's all-black drawing from 1972, and I still have it. And I remember someone saying, it feels so dark and lonely, but I didn't feel that at all, not in the least. I still don't feel that. I often thought he had a dark studio, I remember the dark studio in the 1970s and even when he got up to the country, he closed off the light—he'd show you a tree outside he might say "that's the tree I'm drawing now." I'm always amused when I think of the day I went up with Eliza, the curator at the Phillips Collection, and Jake took us out to his studio, sat us down, the two chairs, closed the door and said okay don't talk, and Eliza and I were sitting there looking at a painting, and it was like he wanted us to ride the wave into the painting—and he was standing there right behind us! One day on the phone he said, "I made a big breakthrough in my painting," he's telling me this on the phone and I'm thinking, oh God I'll drive up there and probably not even notice some tiny difference in a painting but for him was a big breakthrough, and I think what the hell did he do? I know he's already swimming upstream and I'm already trying to catch up. He said to me once, when I was looking a long time at one of his new paintings, "I can see you're trying to figure something out so stop trying to do that." I've always been amused by that. But that was Jake through and through, don't you think?

We each knew we were grateful for each other. We'd worked together a long time. Me as his gallerist—but that's a word I don't like, actually. Gallerist. It's too limited. You know, you work with someone for so many years, it's so much about love and respect and trust, all those big things, and we had those. I remember we went out to dinner—my God, what year was that? And we talked about how we crossed in some very deep and difficult times, with the suicide of Chris Wilmarth—I mean, Jake was a friend that you went through a lot with. Now I have to tell you this: when I started my gallery again in 2004, we went out to dinner. I didn't have a coat so he gave me his coat and we went out to dinner and were hysterical about all the different people we knew and how everything had changed and how everything was exactly the same, and one thing over the years, the years and years, that was always clear, was that Jake felt there needed to be a constancy of devotion to painting but not a constancy to the act of painting, it was full of surprises and digressions and everything else and if you did a big emotional biography of any one painting it would contain all sorts of contradictions because every day of painting was full of emotional contradictions and all sorts of other kinds of contradictions. That may sound simple, but Jake had a complicated mind, and a complicating mind, and they both met some sort of wonderful way together in the paintings, I felt. You know what, I remember him telling me some Old Testament or some phrase or words you told him . . . and it started to show up in our conversations on the phone. . . . "In the hours still left us . . ." He also liked to quote Camus—late in his life, did you know that? "I would rather live my life as if there is a God and die to find out there isn't, than live as if there isn't and to die to find out that there is." I don't know . . . but I feel that Jake chose a path, he was committed to a path, he was always asking questions. He liked the Talmudic path, in a sense . . . you just keep asking questions and you don't ever really give answers, at least not to yourself. When it came to his work I think he felt if he'd found answers he'd stop painting. . . . I have to think about this more, we should talk about this more.

BETTY CUNNINGHAM

RECORDED SUMMER 2023

ACKNOWLEDGMENTS

T his brief memoir could not exist without the rich memories and signature generosity of Betty Cunningham. To my friends and close readers: Bill Barrette in Vermont and Olivia Camilleri in Bologna, thank you for the conversations and encouragement.

ABOUT THE AUTHOR

Howard Norman is the author of novels, memoirs, and books for children. Twice a finalist for the National Book Award in fiction, he received the Lannan Award in Literature. He is completing *Rain Enters My Diary*, a collection of letters sent from Japan to poet W. S. Merwin, an epistolary biography of a friendship. Mr. Norman lives in Vermont.